STEPS TO WRITING SUCCESS

LEVEL 2 Writing Paragraphs

28 Step-by-Step Writing Project Lesson Plans

Written by
June Hetzel, Ph.D., and Deborah Taylor, M.A.

Editor: Teri L. Fisch
Illustrator: Ann Iosa
Cover Illustrator: David Willardson
Designer/Production: Moonhee Pak/Carrie Carter
Cover Designer: Moonhee Pak
Art Director: Tom Cochrane
Project Director: Carolea Williams

Table of Contents

Introduction

Successful writers identify themselves as authors with legitimate voices capable of expressing valuable messages. The lessons in *Steps to Writing Success: Level 2* are designed to help you guide your students towards viewing themselves as authors and taking ownership of their writing. Use the real-world ideas in this book to encourage students to develop a respect for writing, take pride in their work, and become self-reflective, lifelong writers. Enhance this process by providing opportunities for students to read their stories aloud to their classmates in an Author's Chair, publish their stories in class anthologies or weekly newsletters, and share their stories with other students within the school. The lessons in this book teach skills that are commonly found in most language arts standards. Refer to the Scope and Sequence on page 7 to link lessons to the language arts standards your school, district, or state requires.

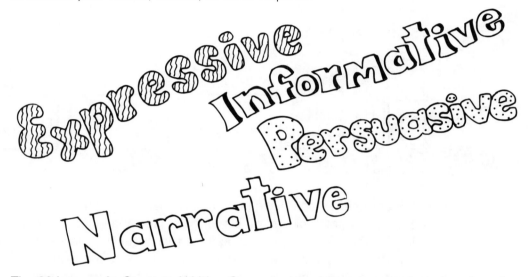

The 28 lessons in *Steps to Writing Success: Level 2* explore the four domains of writing: informative, expressive, narrative, and persuasive. In **informative writing,** students learn to write topic sentences, detail sentences, and closing statements through sequencing, summarizing, and writing about different topics. In **expressive writing,** they learn to use literary devices to express their feelings and observations. In **narrative writing,** students learn to tell a story by developing setting, characters, conflict, resolution, and dialogue. In **persuasive writing,** they learn to convince an audience of their opinion by organizing their arguments.

Use the lessons in this resource to teach students how to create a variety of writing products that reflect all four writing domains—an important skill that students rarely practice in the elementary grades. Students will learn to use the writing process to effectively produce paragraphs. This book is designed to encourage students to extend their writing beyond stories, to writing they can apply to real-life situations and experiences. Encourage students to publish each piece of writing in a creative manner. Suggestions for publishing are included in the Presentation section of each lesson. In addition, the writing templates at the end of the book provide students with fun paper to publish their work. You will be amazed at how your students' writing abilities and confidence soar as they experience success in writing across the four domains.

Overview of the Writing Process

The writing process itself occurs in five stages: prewriting, drafting, revising, editing, and publishing.

Prewriting involves a structured brainstorming session meant to elicit spontaneous thinking about a specific topic. This stage occurs before formal writing. Students generally record and arrange the ideas or information generated during prewriting on a graphic organizer.

The **rough draft** is the second stage, but it is actually the "first round" of writing. During this stage, encourage students to write spontaneously about the information on the graphic organizer. Students should not be overly concerned with spelling at this stage, although their writing does need to be readable.

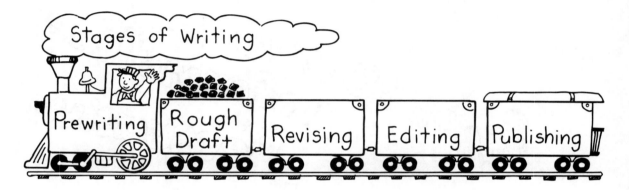

During the **revising** stage, have students evaluate their writing on four levels: entire piece, paragraph or stanza, sentence or line, and word. Ask students to carefully consider the "big picture" as they rearrange or revise text to clarify meaning. They should also review their work to make sure it satisfies the requirements of the writing lesson (as defined by the corresponding rubric). Provide an opportunity for students to give and receive feedback during a "read around." Have students sit in a circle and, on your cue, pass their paper to the right until each student has read six to eight different papers and written suggestions for revisions on the back of each paper. You will notice an increase in the quality of students' writing when they incorporate peer feedback.

After students revise their papers, they are ready for **editing.** This stage involves checking for correct spelling, punctuation, capitalization, and sentence structure. Ask students to focus on the composition of sentences to make sure they are grammatically correct, are not missing words, and do not contain extraneous words. Encourage students to use the rubric on page 8 to edit their work. Enhance the editing process by having students ask a classmate and you (or another adult) to use the rubric to evaluate their writing.

After the editing stage is complete, students move into **publishing** their work as a final draft. This is often the most rewarding stage for students because it is at this point that writers can finally see their completed work in a polished form and can share it with their classmates.

A Note about Spelling

Students should not focus on spelling during the initial draft and revision stages of their writing. Ask them to focus only on clearly communicating their ideas. However, once the ideas are refined, correct spelling is critical so the audience can enjoy the writing. Unfortunately, students regularly struggle with spelling. Use the following ideas to address spelling during the writing process:

- Sticky Notes: Walk around the room with sticky notes as students are writing. When students ask how to spell a word, quickly write it on a sticky note, and place the note on their desk.
- Try It Cards: Give each student a stack of index cards held together with a metal ring. Instead of telling students to raise their hand when they need help with a word, ask them to simply write a "best guess" for the spelling on a "Try It Card." Verify or correct each student's spellings as you walk around the room.

- Personalized Dictionaries: A personalized dictionary can simply be a spiral binder. Have students label every other page with a letter of the alphabet and record words that stumped them in the spelling process. Over time, students will collect important writing words and create a ready reference tool.

Encourage students to look up hard-to-spell words in a published dictionary such as *Scholastic Children's Dictionary* (Scholastic) and add correct spellings to their personalized dictionary for easy reference.

- Word Walls: Word walls meet the collective spelling needs of a classroom. To make a word wall, post the alphabet on the classroom wall, write key spelling and vocabulary words on index cards, and display each card beneath the letter of the alphabet that matches the first letter of the word.
- Sight Word Lists: Every student needs access to the words most commonly used in writing. Generally, students use sight word lists (e.g., Dolch or Fry). Systematic study of high-frequency words can only benefit young writers. Highlight these words in personalized dictionaries or on word walls.

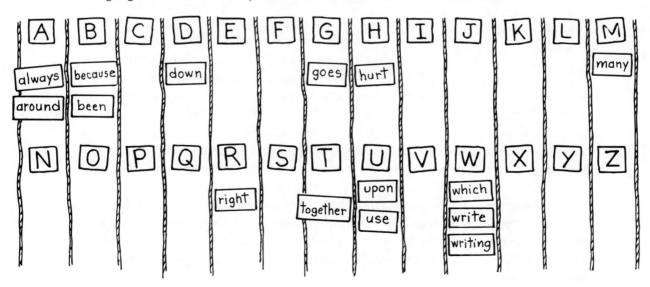

Lesson Overview

Steps to Writing Success: Level 2 features easy-to-follow, comprehensive lesson plans for helping students complete 28 writing projects, with seven lessons focusing on each of the domains: informative, expressive, narrative, and persuasive. Each lesson lists the objective and critical components of the writing project and includes detailed directions for preparing all the required materials and preliminary activities that will engage students' interest and build background knowledge. (Typical classroom materials such as scissors, crayons, markers, glue, and writing paper and materials needed for the Presentation ideas are not listed in the Preparation section.) Each lesson also provides explicit steps for direct instruction, guided practice, and independent practice; suggested ways for students to present their writing projects; teaching tips; and cross-curricular student activities. Each lesson includes a writing template with pictures and borders that relate to the theme of the lesson. These will help motivate students as they write their final drafts. The book includes one rubric that clarifies the requirements and expectations for the writing projects. For each lesson, you will need to fill in the critical components, which are located at the beginning of the lesson. The rubrics will help students focus their writing, develop revision and editing skills, and be more accountable in their writing.

Preceding Week
- Preparation
  - ✔ Read aloud books
  - ✔ Gather materials
  - ✔ Photocopy reproducibles
  - ✔ Make transparencies

Day 1
- Setting the Stage
- Instructional Input

Day 2
- Guided Practice
- Independent Practice
  - ✔ Hand out rubric

Days 3–5
- Independent Practice continues
- Presentation
- Assign journal prompts

Each lesson in *Steps to Writing Success: Level 2* should be taught within three to five days. Prepare for each lesson by reviewing the Preparation section during the preceding week. Read aloud the books listed or others with similar content to introduce students to the topic that will be the focus of the writing lesson. Many of these are picture books because they help students at every level quickly and clearly identify the elements of good writing. Set up comfortable areas with pillows, beanbag chairs, and carpet pieces to create a relaxed and enjoyable environment. On the first day of the lesson, implement the activities from the Setting the Stage section, and then proceed with the Instructional Input activity that follows. On the second day, begin the Guided Practice activity with your class, and then assign the Independent Practice activity. Give each student a rubric at the beginning of the Independent Practice activity so students are aware of the requirements of the writing project and your expectations before they begin to write. Students should complete the Independent Practice and the Presentation sections within two to three days, depending on the requirements of the project. Use the prompts at the end of the list of Teaching Hints/Extensions to provide ideas for daily journal writing. Encourage students to count the number of words they write each day, and have them record this data on a graph for self-feedback. Your students will feel a strong sense of accomplishment and be motivated to continue writing as they watch the number of words on their graphs grow.

Scope and Sequence

The skills listed on the chart represent those commonly found in most language arts standards.

Lesson Title	Complete Sentences	Paragraph Structure	Topic Sentences	Supporting Details	Capitalization	Ending Punctuation	Quotation Marks	Sequencing	
Creature Feature	●	●	●	●	●	●		●	Informative
Circus, Circus	●	●	●	●	●	●		●	Informative
Picnic in the Park	●	●	●	●	●	●		●	Informative
Cool Cones	●	●	●	●	●	●		●	Informative
Community Helpers	●	●	●	●	●	●		●	Informative
Simply Summaries	●	●	●	●	●	●		●	Informative
Body Builders	●	●	●	●	●	●		●	Informative
Silly Similes	●				●	●			Expressive
Alliteration Acrobatics	●				●	●			Expressive
Countless Colors	●	●	●	●	●	●		●	Expressive
Auditory Antics	●	●	●	●	●	●		●	Expressive
Food Festival	●	●	●	●	●	●		●	Expressive
Kinesthetic Clues	●	●	●	●	●	●		●	Expressive
Fantastic Feelings	●				●	●			Expressive
Postcard Dreams	●	●	●	●	●	●		●	Narrative
Friendship Circle	●	●	●	●	●	●		●	Narrative
Mirror, Mirror	●	●	●	●	●	●		●	Narrative
Pictures from the Past	●	●	●	●	●	●		●	Narrative
Once Upon a Time	●	●	●	●	●	●		●	Narrative
Walkie-Talkie	●				●	●	●	●	Narrative
Dialogue Dynamics	●				●	●	●	●	Narrative
Ordering Arguments	●	●	●	●	●	●		●	Persuasive
Commercial Interruption	●	●	●	●	●	●	●	●	Persuasive
Big-Time Books	●	●	●	●	●	●		●	Persuasive
Marvelous Movies	●	●	●	●	●	●	●	●	Persuasive
Restaurant Raves	●	●	●	●	●	●		●	Persuasive
Invention Convention	●	●	●	●	●	●		●	Persuasive
Amusement Fun	●	●	●	●	●	●		●	Persuasive

Author's Name _____ Date _____

Peer Evaluator's Name _____

Rubric

	I think			My classmate thinks			My teacher thinks		
	☹ 😐 🙂			☹ 😐 🙂			☹ 😐 🙂		
Critical Components									
Revising and Editing									
Did I make changes if I had new ideas?									
Did I make corrections if I made mistakes?									
Mechanics									
Did I write complete sentences?									
Did I remember to indent my paragraph?									
Did I use correct capitalization?									
Did I use correct punctuation?									
Did I spell correctly?									

I liked _____

_____ .

The best part was _____

_____ .

An area to improve is _____

_____ .

Steps to Writing Success: Level 2 © 2002 Creative Teaching Press

Creature Feature

Preparation

Read aloud books about animals.

- *Amazing Snakes (Eyewitness Juniors)* by Alexandra Parsons (Alfred A. Knopf Books)
- *How to Hide an Octopus and Other Sea Creatures* by Ruth Heller (Putnam)
- *The Icky Bug Alphabet Book* by Jerry Pallotta (Charlesbridge Publishing)

Gather 20 to 30 nonfiction animal books for the classroom library.

Write three to four paragraphs, each with a topic sentence that states what the paragraph is about.

Make copies of these reproducibles.
- Sample Paragraph Puzzles (page 12) transparency
- Creature Paragraph Puzzles (page 13) one photocopy for every two students
- Creature Brainstorm (page 14) transparency, class set of photocopies
- writing template (page 15) transparency, class set of photocopies
- rubric (page 8) transparency, class set of photocopies

Cut apart the Creature Paragraph Puzzles (page 13), and put each set of pieces in a separate envelope.

OBJECTIVE

The student will write

a topic sentence.

CRITICAL COMPONENTS

- The topic sentence contains the main idea of the paragraph.

- Complete sentences are written with correct capitalization and punctuation.

- The paragraph is indented.

Setting the Stage

Share the following riddles with the class:

I have eight legs and two body parts. I have many eyes. I have a red hourglass on my belly. What am I? (black widow)

I have a long brown and tan body. I have a forked tongue. I slither on the ground. My tail has a rattle on the end. What am I? (rattlesnake)

I am a type of bird. I am very small. My feathers shimmer in the sun. I am green and red and black. I fly like a helicopter. What am I? (hummingbird)

After students identify each animal, have them say a sentence about the animal that incorporates the clues in the riddle. For example, a student might say *A hummingbird is a colorful bird that flies like a helicopter.* Ask students to make up their own riddles and share them with the class.

Instructional Input

1 Discuss what a topic is with the class. Explain that a paragraph is five or more sentences about one topic and that it begins with a topic sentence that states what the paragraph is about (the main idea). Show students the examples of paragraphs you wrote. Discuss the topic sentence of each paragraph.

2 Display the Sample Paragraph Puzzles overhead transparency. Cover the paragraphs with a piece of paper so only the topic sentences are showing. Read them aloud, and define them as topic sentences. Uncover the paragraphs on the transparency, and read them aloud.

3 Ask students to identify which topic sentence goes with each paragraph, and then read aloud each complete paragraph. Ask the following questions to help students determine if they are correct: *How do you know this topic sentence goes with this paragraph? When we read the whole paragraph, including the topic sentence, does it make sense? Why?* Emphasize the concept of main idea and staying on topic.

4 Give each pair of students an envelope with a set of Creature Paragraph Puzzles in it. Invite them to try to correctly identify the paragraph that belongs with each topic sentence. Ask volunteers to share their answers with the class.

Guided Practice

1 Have the class research an animal from one of the following categories: Furry Friends, Feathery Friends, Radical Reptiles, or Fishy Fish. Divide the class into small groups. Invite groups to look through nonfiction animal books to collect information and record it on paper.

2 Display the Creature Brainstorm overhead transparency. Ask students to help you fill in the information. With the class's help, write a paragraph about the creature on the board or chart paper. Read it aloud, and have the class revise and edit it.

3 Write a final draft of the paragraph on the writing template overhead transparency. Display the rubric overhead transparency. Ask the class to help you evaluate the paragraph and discuss further changes that can be made.

Independent Practice

1 Have each student choose an animal research category and then browse through books to gather information about a specific animal or an entire group of animals.

2 Give each student a Creature Brainstorm reproducible. Have students complete it and then copy the information in paragraph form on lined paper to create their rough draft paragraph.

3 Have students revise and edit their rough draft and then use the rubric to evaluate their writing.

Presentation

- Have students **publish** their final drafts and illustrations on the writing template reproducible.

- Have students **create** three-dimensional clay or Styrofoam models of animals.

- **Display** student work on a bulletin board titled *Creature Features*, and place students' animal models on a table near the bulletin board. Tape magazine pictures of animals around the bulletin board as a border.

TEACHING HINTS/EXTENSIONS

- Invite students to use colored overhead pens to draw their animals on overhead transparencies. Have them display their drawings while they read aloud their paragraphs.

- Have students create riddles about animals. Ask them to write their riddles on index cards, with the answer on the back. Place the cards on a metal ring, and use them as a "sponge" activity before lunch or at the end of the day.

- Invite students to write self-checking "creature cards" on large index cards. Have them write a topic sentence and a paragraph that concludes with a question about the animal. Encourage students to write the answer on the back. Place the cards on a low bulletin board with pushpins so students can read each card, guess the answer, remove the card, and then turn it over to see if they were correct.

- Have students complete one or more of these writing prompts in a journal:
  - ✔ Write a topic sentence for a paragraph about your family.
  - ✔ Write a topic sentence for a paragraph about your favorite friend.
  - ✔ Write a topic sentence for a paragraph about a birthday surprise.

Sample Paragraph Puzzles

Frogs	Lizards	Snakes
are amphibians.	are reptiles.	are interesting.

Frogs

They live in the water and on land in swamps or ponds. They have long back legs to help them leap far. When they are born, they are called tadpoles. Sometimes, they are green in color.

Lizards

They have long bodies but no legs. They are covered with dry scales. They live in deserts, forests, oceans, streams, and lakes. One of the largest is the anaconda that lives in South America.

Snakes

They are cold-blooded animals that live in deserts. Their skin is dry and scaly. They hatch from eggs. They are related to snakes.

Steps to Writing Success: Level 2 © 2002 Creative Teaching Press

Creature Paragraph Puzzles

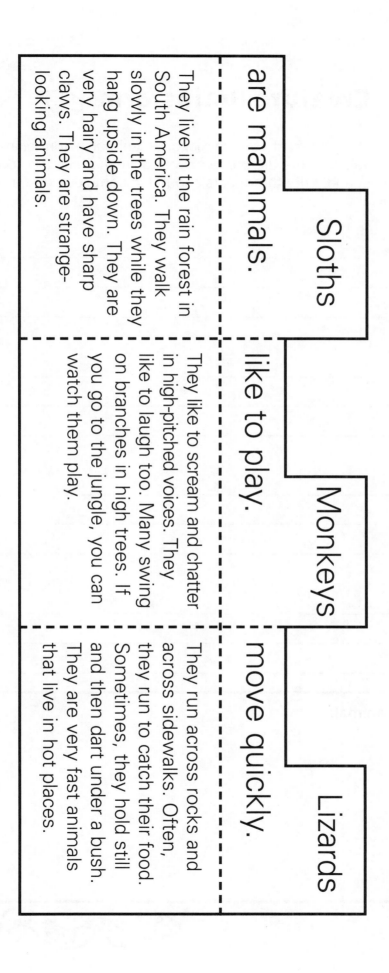

Sloths
are mammals.

They live in the rain forest in South America. They walk slowly in the trees while they hang upside down. They are very hairy and have sharp claws. They are strange-looking animals.

Monkeys
like to play.

They like to scream and chatter in high-pitched voices. They like to laugh too. Many swing on branches in high trees. If you go to the jungle, you can watch them play.

Lizards
move quickly.

They run across rocks and across sidewalks. Often, they run to catch their food. Sometimes, they hold still and then dart under a bush. They are very fast animals that live in hot places.

Name _____   Date _____

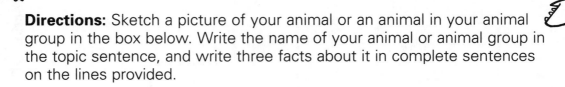

Creature Brainstorm

Directions: Sketch a picture of your animal or an animal in your animal group in the box below. Write the name of your animal or animal group in the topic sentence, and write three facts about it in complete sentences on the lines provided.

Topic Sentence: _____

_____

_____

Fact #1: _____

_____

_____

Fact #2: _____

_____

_____

Fact #3: _____

_____

_____

Sketch your animal.

Steps to Writing Success: Level 2 © 2002 Creative Teaching Press

By

Circus, Circus

Preparation

Read aloud books about the circus or zoo.

- *Curious George Visits the Zoo* by Margret and H. A. Rey (Houghton Mifflin)
- *Felix Joins the Circus* by Annette Langen (Abbeville Press)
- *If I Ran the Circus* by Dr. Seuss (Random House)

Gather 20 to 30 books about the circus and zoo for the classroom library.

Take the class to a circus (optional field trip).

Make copies of these reproducibles.
- Detail Paragraphs (page 19) transparency
- Circus Brainstorm (page 20) transparency, class set of photocopies
- writing template (page 21) class set of photocopies
- rubric (page 8) class set of photocopies

Setting the Stage

Ask students to tell you about the animals they might see at a circus or zoo, and record their ideas on the board. Encourage students to share details about each animal.

Instructional Input

1 Ask students what details are. Have a volunteer stand. Ask the class to share details about him or her.

OBJECTIVE

The student will write at least three supporting detail sentences in a paragraph about a circus animal.

CRITICAL COMPONENTS

- Detail sentences add more information about the topic.

- Complete sentences are written with correct capitalization and punctuation.

- The paragraph is indented.

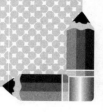

2 Tell the class that you went to the circus and saw a *wump*. Explain to students that a wump is a made-up animal but that you can help them picture it in their heads by telling details about it. Tell the class what the wump looks like, what it acts like, and what it eats. Ask if these details helped them visualize the wump even though it is not a real animal.

3 Display the Detail Paragraphs overhead transparency. Read aloud the paragraphs. Ask students to explain the difference between the two paragraphs. Discuss why the boy in the second picture can see the koala in his mind but the boy in the first picture can't.

Guided Practice

1 Display the Circus Brainstorm overhead transparency. Ask a volunteer to choose a circus animal and draw it on the transparency.

2 Ask volunteers to share three details about the animal. Record their responses.

3 Write a paragraph about this circus animal on the board or chart paper. Use the information from the transparency to guide you as you write a topic sentence and three detail sentences.

> Today I saw an elephant at the circus. The elephant was big and gray. It had extremely large ears that flapped when it ran. Its nose, or trunk, was long. It could carry things with its trunk and shoot water from its trunk.

Independent Practice

1 Invite each student to find an interesting circus or animal book in the classroom library. Have students look through it for about 5 minutes and then choose an animal. Ask students to share which animal they chose.

2 Give each student a Circus Brainstorm reproducible. Ask students to draw a sketch of their animal and write three details about it.

3 Invite students to use the information they recorded to write a rough draft paragraph about their animal.

4 Have students revise and edit their rough draft and then use the rubric to evaluate their writing.

● Have students **publish** their final drafts on the writing template reproducible and mount them on construction paper. Invite students to draw an illustration on a separate piece of paper.

● **Display** student work on a bulletin board titled *Circus, Circus Everywhere.*

Circus, Circus Everywhere

TEACHING HINTS/EXTENSIONS

● This lesson does not emphasize the closing summary statement of the paragraph. Therefore, review the previous lesson on topic sentences, and wait for the next lesson to place emphasis on a closing statement.

● Always have books about animals in the classroom library. Students can use them for a multitude of writing lessons and extended assignments, including writing animal reports, creating animal puppet plays based on animal facts, and writing animal stories.

● Collect videos on animals. (National Geographic has a good collection.) Show a short piece of the video on a particular animal, discuss it, and then have students write a paragraph with many detail sentences that describe what they remember from the video.

● Have students complete one or more of these writing prompts in a journal:
  ✔ Write a paragraph that includes details about your favorite dessert.
  ✔ Write a paragraph that includes details about a favorite book.
  ✔ Write a paragraph that includes details about a pet you would like to have.

Detail Paragraphs

Without Details

    I saw a koala at the zoo. It was interesting. I like koalas.

With Details

    I saw a koala at the zoo. It was from Australia. It was eating leaves in a eucalyptus tree. It was gray and white and about the size of my dog. It looked so sweet that I wanted to hold it, but the zookeeper said that koalas can be mean. Seeing my first koala at the zoo was exciting!

Steps to Writing Success: Level 2 © 2002 Creative Teaching Press

Circus Brainstorm

Name _____ Date _____

Directions: Sketch a picture of an animal you could see at the circus. Write the name of the animal and three details about it on the lines provided.

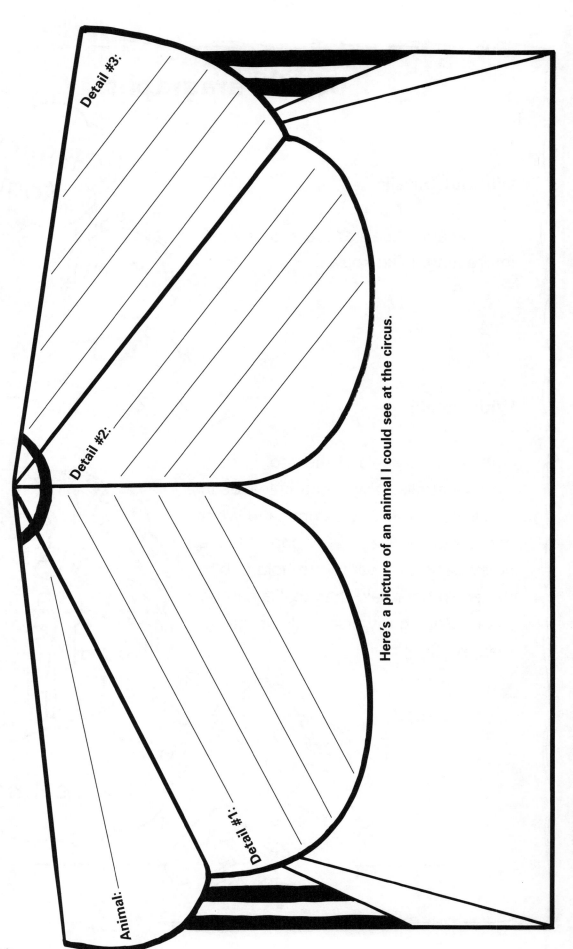

Detail #3: _____

Detail #2: _____

Detail #1: _____

Animal: _____

Here's a picture of an animal I could see at the circus.

Steps to Writing Success: Level 2 © 2002 Creative Teaching Press

By

Steps to Writing Success: Level 2 © 2002 Creative Teaching Press

Picnic in the Park

Preparation

Read aloud books about parks or picnics.

- *Peewee's Tale* by Johanna Hurwitz (Sea Star Books)
- *A Picnic in October* by Eve Bunting (Harcourt)
- *Stella and Roy* by Ashley Wolff (Dutton)

Gather three different colored overhead pens.

Write three to four paragraphs, each with a closing statement that restates what the paragraph is about (the main idea from the topic sentence).

Plan a class picnic at a local park (optional field trip).

Make copies of these reproducibles.
- Sample Paragraphs (page 25) transparency
- Closing Puzzles (page 26) one photocopy for every two students
- Closing Statements (page 27) class set of photocopies
- Picnic Brainstorm (page 28) class set of photocopies
- writing template (page 29) class set of photocopies
- rubric (page 8) class set of photocopies

Cut apart the Closing Puzzles (page 26), and put each set of pieces in a separate envelope.

Setting the Stage

Take your class to a local park for a picnic and games, or set up the picnic on your school's play field. If inclement weather or conditions prevent this, move desks and tables to the perimeters of your classroom. Lay some blankets on the floor, and invite students to eat their lunch "picnic style." While they eat, talk about why picnics are fun. Share stories about picnics you have gone on. Invite students to share their own picnic stories.

OBJECTIVE

The student will write a closing statement at the end of an informative paragraph.

CRITICAL COMPONENTS

- The closing statement summarizes or repeats the theme of the topic sentence.

- Complete sentences are written with correct capitalization and punctuation.

- The paragraph is indented.

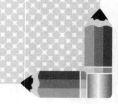

Instructional Input

1 Invite students to close their eyes and imagine what they might do on a picnic. Encourage them to share their ideas. Record their responses on the board. Point out that these are details about the topic picnic.

2 Review paragraph structure (topic and detail sentences) with the class. Tell them that paragraphs always end with a closing statement that restates the main idea from the topic sentence. Show students the examples of paragraphs you wrote. Discuss the closing statement of each paragraph.

3 Display the Sample Paragraphs overhead transparency. Read aloud each paragraph. Ask volunteers to circle or underline each topic sentence, the detail sentences, and each closing statement with a different colored overhead pen.

4 Discuss each paragraph, and point out the relationship between the topic sentence and the closing statement. Show how they both contain the main idea but use different words to express it.

Guided Practice

1 Give each pair of students an envelope with a set of Closing Puzzles in it. Invite them to read the paragraphs and identify which closing statement finishes each paragraph.

2 Ask volunteers to share their answers with the class. Have them discuss why the closing statement goes with the paragraph.

3 Review how to write closing statements. Give each student a Closing Statements reproducible, and read aloud the directions.

4 After all students have completed their work, have several volunteers share the closing statement they wrote for each paragraph. Emphasize the importance of rewriting the main idea to create a closing statement.

Independent Practice

1 Invite students to think about a time or imagine a time that they enjoyed a picnic in the park. Ask each student to share one detail about his or her picnic.

2 Give each student a Picnic Brainstorm reproducible. Have students draw a picture of their picnic and then record a setting, three details about it, and a closing thought.

3 Have students use the information they recorded to write a rough draft paragraph.

4 Have students revise and edit their rough draft and then use the rubric to evaluate their writing.

Presentation

- Have students **publish** their final drafts and illustrations on the writing template reproducible or on a brown paper bag.

- **Display** student work on a bulletin board titled *A Picnic in the Park* with a tablecloth or blanket as the backdrop. Encourage students to cut out black construction paper ants, and tape them to the bulletin board.

TEACHING HINTS/EXTENSIONS

- Invite students to expand their paragraphs and write lengthier stories. Publish the collection as a class book titled *Picnic Tales: Stories to Munch On*.

- Invite students to browse through magazines and cut out stand-alone paragraphs that show examples of closing statements that restate the main idea. Have them glue these paragraphs into a scrapbook titled *Closing Statements*. Periodically, check the collection and use the paragraphs as springboards for additional mini-lessons.

- Read aloud *One Hundred Hungry Ants* by Elinor J. Pinczes (Houghton Mifflin). Invite students to write similar stories with their own events and rhyme.

- Have students complete one or more of these writing prompts in a journal:
  - ✔ Write a paragraph about a bird. Remember to tell what type of bird you are writing about and include a closing statement.
  - ✔ Write a paragraph about school. Include a topic sentence, three to five detail sentences, and a closing statement.
  - ✔ Write a paragraph about your favorite gift. Include a topic sentence, three to five detail sentences, and a closing statement.

Sample Paragraphs

Yopi Park

A picnic in Yopi Park is an exciting event. We like to picnic near the Metap River. We hear the water rushing by us. The air is cool and crisp. We can see Yopi Falls from where we eat. The smell of pine is wonderful. A picnic in Yopi Park is like a dream.

Beautiful Roses

Roses are beautiful. You must prune them in the winter. You also must fertilize the ground. After waiting a long time, the flowers begin to grow. Then you see the buds. When the flowers bloom, they are so pretty and unforgettable.

Soccer—A Fun Game

Soccer is a fun and exhausting game. You need several people to play on each team. You need to have a goal and a goalie for each side. You kick the ball with your feet. You can even use your head—but not your hands! In soccer, you run a lot. When you score a goal, all the running is worth it. Soccer is an enjoyable but tiring game.

Closing Puzzles

Teacher Directions: Carefully cut apart the closing statements and paragraphs. Place each set of six pieces in an envelope.

The Gray Whale

California

gray whales are the size of a school bus. They travel in groups called pods. They swim along California's coast. They have their babies in the warm waters of Baja Mexico.

Everyone enjoys seeing the huge gray whales swim by.

Hunny Beach

Hunny Beach

is a fun beach I like to go to when I am in New Jersey. It is large and flat. White sand covers the beach. Most days are warm in the summer. However, winter can be cold and windy.

This beach is an interesting place to visit.

Tide Pools

Tide pools

are fun to explore during low tide. Small pools of water gather in the rocks. You can easily see small fish and other sea animals. Sea stars and mussels are a few of the animals you can see.

You will enjoy viewing tide pools at low tide.

Steps to Writing Success: Level 2 © 2002 Creative Teaching Press

Closing Statements

Name _____   Date _____

Directions: Read the paragraphs. Write a closing statement for each paragraph. Be sure the closing statement restates the main idea from the topic sentence.

I like to swim. I swim in my pool. I swim at the YMCA. I also swim in the ocean.

_____
_____
_____
_____
_____

Basketball is my favorite sport. I enjoy all of the running. I am a good shot. I can even shoot free throws. I practice basketball with my friends.

_____
_____
_____
_____
_____

It is important to take care of your pets. They need food and water. They need a collar. They need to be groomed. They need to be loved.

_____
_____
_____
_____
_____

Name _____

Date _____

Picnic Brainstorm

Directions: Draw a picture of what you did on your picnic. Write the setting, three details, and a closing thought about your picnic.

Setting: _____

Detail #3: _____

Detail #1: _____

Detail #2: _____

Draw what you did on your picnic.

Closing: _____

Steps to Writing Success: Level 2 © 2002 Creative Teaching Press

By

Cool Cones

Preparation

Read aloud books that tell a sequenced story.

- *Jumanji* by Chris Van Allsburg (Houghton Mifflin)
- *Millions of Cats* by Wanda Gag (Putnam)
- *The Snowy Day* by Ezra Jack Keats (Viking)

Gather *Grandfather's Journey* by Allan Say (Houghton Mifflin).

Create four ice-cream containers by covering coffee cans with construction paper and labeling them *chocolate, vanilla, strawberry*, and *other flavors*.

Make copies of these reproducibles.
- Cone and Bowl Patterns (page 33) class set of photocopies, teacher photocopy
- Scoop Patterns (page 34) class set of photocopies on brown, cream, pink, and white construction paper
- _____'s Cool Ice Cream (page 35) class set of photocopies
- rubric (page 8) class set of photocopies

Cut out the Cone and Bowl Patterns (page 33) and Scoop Patterns (page 34). Place each set of scoop cutouts in the matching ice-cream container.

Setting the Stage

Display the ice-cream containers with the scoops inside. Invite students to choose their favorite ice-cream flavor and take a scoop from that container. Write the four container titles on the board. Invite students to tape their scoop under the correct title. Ask students who chose "other flavors" to write the flavor name next to their scoop. Count the scoops, and ask questions about them such as *Which flavor is the most popular? How many students chose that flavor?*

chocolate	strawberry
![choc scoops]	![strawberry scoops]
vanilla	other flavors
![vanilla scoops]	🍥 rocky road 🍥 mint chip 🍥 peppermint

OBJECTIVE

The student will write a paragraph of simple sequenced sentences that explain how to make an ice-cream sundae or cone.

CRITICAL COMPONENTS

- Sentences are written in chronological order.
- The paragraph has a topic sentence and a closing statement.
- The paragraph includes ordinal words.

Instructional Input

1 Ask students to think of ordinal words (e.g., *first, second, third*) and sequence words (e.g., *then, after that, finally*). Record their responses on the board or on chart paper.

2 Read aloud *Grandfather's Journey.* Have students use ordinal words and sequence words to retell the story.

3 Have students use ordinal words in a variety of activities. For example, have four students stand at the door. Ask the class who is first in line, second in line, third in line, and last in line. Invite students to explain the order in which they perform a task such as brushing their teeth or washing the dishes.

4 Discuss why it is important to use words like *first, second,* and *third* when explaining how to do things.

Guided Practice

1 Have the class help you write the directions for making an ice-cream sundae or a double-dip ice-cream cone. Tape an ice-cream bowl or ice-cream cone cutout on the board, and use the construction paper ice-cream scoops to build the sundae or cone as you write the directions.

2 Write a topic sentence (e.g., *This is how you make an ice-cream sundae*) on the board. Then, ask a volunteer to tell you what you need to do first (e.g., *First, I get an ice-cream bowl*). Record the response on the board under the ice-cream bowl or cone.

3 Ask what you do next, and record the responses (e.g., *Second, I get a scoop of chocolate ice cream. Third, I get a scoop of vanilla*). Tape scoops on the bowl or cone, and label them with the correct flavor as you write each step. Write a closing statement for your directions (e.g., *This is how you put together a delicious ice-cream sundae*).

4 Have the class read aloud the directions. Discuss whether all of the necessary steps are included.

Independent Practice

1 Invite students to write their own sequenced directions for how to make an ice-cream sundae or a double-dip ice-cream cone. Tell them to list the steps in the correct order.

2 Tell students to write their steps in paragraph form. Remind them to use ordinal words and include a topic sentence, at least three steps, and a closing statement.

3 Have students revise and edit their rough draft and then use the rubric to evaluate their writing.

- Have students **publish** their final drafts on the _____'s Cool Ice Cream reproducible and mount them on construction paper.

- Have students **build** an ice-cream sundae or a double-dip ice-cream cone using the cutouts from the Cone and Bowl Patterns and Scoop Patterns reproducibles.

- **Display** student work on a bulletin board titled *"Cool" Cones*.

TEACHING HINTS/EXTENSIONS

- Use the scoops to reinforce concepts related to graphing, addition, subtraction, more than, less than, and counting.

- Invite students to write recipes to create a new flavor of ice cream. For example, students might mix chocolate chips, cherries, nuts, and marshmallows into vanilla ice cream. Display the writing on a bulletin board titled *Here's the Scoop!* As students write, encourage them to use ordinal words.

- Design a learning center activity titled Ice-Cream Match. Write pairs of synonyms on cones and scoops. Make them self-checking by writing the matching word backwards on the back of each piece. Challenge students to stretch their vocabulary by matching the synonyms.

- Have students complete one or more of these writing prompts in a journal:
    - ✔ Write a paragraph that tells how to get from school to your home. Use ordinal words. Don't skip any steps.
    - ✔ Write a paragraph that tells the order of how to get ready for school.
    - ✔ Write a paragraph about three wishes you have been granted by a genie. Use ordinal words to tell about them.

Cone and Bowl Patterns

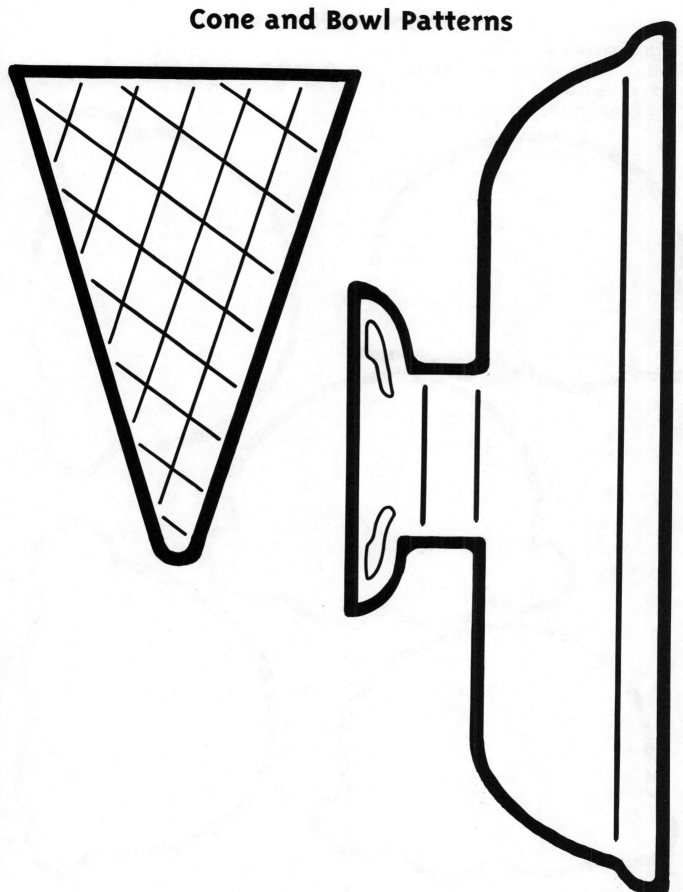

Scoop Patterns

Teacher Directions: Make enough copies of this reproducible on brown (chocolate), cream (vanilla), pink (strawberry), and white (other flavors) construction paper so that you have a class set of ice-cream scoops in each color. Cut out the scoops, and put each set of scoops in the corresponding ice-cream container.

Steps to Writing Success: Level 2 © 2002 Creative Teaching Press

_____'s Cool Ice Cream

Steps to Writing Success: Level 2 © 2002 Creative Teaching Press

Community Helpers

Preparation

Read aloud books about community helpers.

- *Community Helpers From A–Z* by Bobbie D. Kalman (Crabtree)
- *Fire Fighters* by Angela Royston (DK Publishing)
- *A Police Officer . . . That's What I'll Be* by Ronald Pinkston (Pinkston Publishing)

Gather two pieces of chart paper and a collection of community helper props such as hats, a hose, a badge, chalk, a date stamper, a stop sign, a stethoscope, a thermometer, and an envelope.

Make copies of these reproducibles.
- Hospital (page 39) transparency
- Community Helper Brainstorm (page 40) transparency, class set of photocopies
- writing template (page 41) class set of photocopies
- rubric (page 8) class set of photocopies

Setting the Stage

Ask students what kind of job they would like to have when they grow up. Record their responses on chart paper. After you have listed several jobs, circle all the community helper jobs. Ask the class what these jobs have in common. Listen to several responses. Then, explain that the ones you circled are jobs that help other people in a special way and that the people in these jobs are called community helpers. Display the community helper props. Ask students to choose a prop and tell about the job of the person who would use it.

Instructional Input

1 Display the Hospital overhead transparency. Ask students what they see in the illustration. Read aloud the words, and discuss with the class the role of a doctor. Record shared information on another piece of chart paper.

2 Ask students to close their eyes and imagine a time they visited a doctor's office. Have each student share one word about the experience (e.g., shot, nurse, stitches), and add the words to the chart paper.

3 Display the Community Helper Brainstorm overhead transparency. Invite students to help you write about the job of a doctor by completing the information on the transparency. Encourage them to use words listed on the chart paper in addition to the ones in the illustration on the Hospital transparency.

4 Display the Hospital transparency again. Have the class help you write a paragraph that describes the doctor's job. Have them use the information you recorded on the Community Helper Brainstorm transparency and words from the chart paper to develop the paragraph. Write a topic sentence that says the name of the community helper, at least three detail sentences, and a closing statement that restates the main idea of the paragraph.

> Doctor
> — helps people
> — saves lives
> — gives shots
> — has an office
> — nurse
> — works in hospital
> — surgery
> — broken arm
> — stitches

Guided Practice

1 Give each student a Community Helper Brainstorm reproducible. Assign each student a partner. Ask each partner to choose a different community helper from the word bank and circle it.

2 Tell students to turn over their paper and draw a horizontal line across the middle of the paper. Invite them to draw a detailed illustration of their community helper at work above the line. Have them write the names of the objects the community helper uses below the line to create a word bank. Encourage partners to help each other come up with more words.

3 Ask students to use their illustration and word bank to help them fill out the other side of the reproducible. Encourage partners to read aloud their ideas and help each other come up with more ideas.

Independent Practice

1 Invite students to write a rough draft paragraph based on the information they recorded on the reproducible, their illustration, and their word bank.

2 Have students revise and edit their rough draft and then use the rubric to evaluate their writing.

Presentation

- Have students **publish** their final drafts and illustrations of their community helper at work on the writing template reproducible.

- **Invite** students to share their paragraphs with the class. Encourage them to wear clothing or carry props that relate to their community helpers.

- **Bind** student work into a class book titled *Community Helpers at Work.*

TEACHING HINTS/EXTENSIONS

- Invite a local community helper such as a crossing guard, nurse, or firefighter to your classroom. Interview the guest speaker. This will encourage students to write far beyond a mere paragraph.

- Students may know in-depth information about the particular careers of their family members. Invite them to write about one of these jobs.

- In discussing the roles of community helpers and other careers, take the opportunity to reinforce important character qualities that promote success in the workplace, such as kindness, courtesy, patience, thoughtfulness, service to others, friendliness, perseverance, respect, and creativity. Invite students to role-play to show examples of these traits.

- Have students complete one or more of these writing prompts in a journal:
    - ✔ Write a paragraph about your job as a school principal. What kind of principal would you be? What would you do all day? What would you do for your school?
    - ✔ Imagine you are a zookeeper. Write a paragraph about your job. What is the name of your zoo? What kinds of animals live there? What do you do all day as a zookeeper?
    - ✔ Write a paragraph about your job as an elementary school librarian. What would you do all day? How will you make sure the students at your school have wonderful books to read?

Hospital

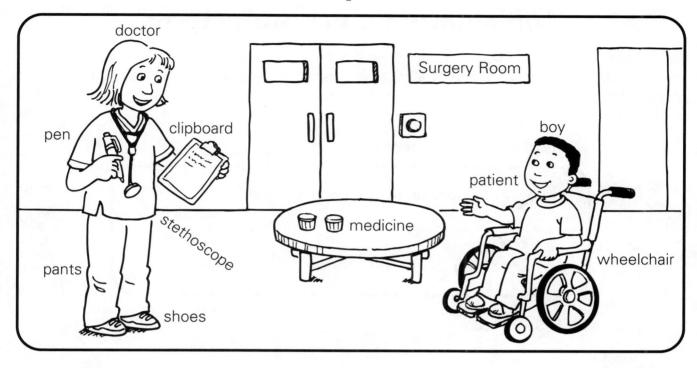

doctor

pen

clipboard

Surgery Room

boy

patient

stethoscope

medicine

pants

wheelchair

shoes

Name _____   Date _____

Community Helper Brainstorm

Directions: Circle the name of a community helper in the word bank. On the back of this paper, draw your community helper at work and list the objects he or she uses. Use the information on the back of your paper to brainstorm a topic sentence, ideas for detail sentences, and a closing statement.

Name of Community Helper: _____

Community Helper Word Bank

firefighter

nurse   letter carrier   librarian

police officer   doctor

crossing guard   teacher   sanitation worker

Topic Sentence: _____

_____

Ideas for Supporting Detail Sentences

What does a _____ do?	What tools does a _____ need?	What training or schooling does a _____ need?	What kind of personality does a _____ need?

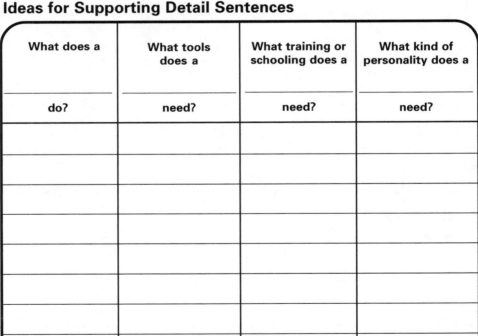

Closing Statement: _____

Steps to Writing Success: Level 2 © 2002 Creative Teaching Press

By
_____

_____

_____

_____

_____

_____

_____

_____

_____

_____

_____

Simply Summaries

Read aloud picture books that can easily be summarized.

- *Chrysanthemum* by Kevin Henkes (Mulberry Books)
- *Make Way for Ducklings* by Robert McCloskey (Viking)
- *Where the Wild Things Are* by Maurice Sendak (HarperCollins)

Gather science books, social studies books, nonfiction books on animals, and encyclopedias, and photocopy passages for students to summarize.

- *Children's Illustrated Encyclopedia* (DK Publishing)
- *The Kingfisher First Animal Encyclopedia* by Jon Kirkwood and John Farndon (Kingfisher Books)
- *Scholastic Encyclopedia of Animals* by Laurence P. Pringle (Scholastic)

Make copies of these reproducibles.

- Playing the Piano (page 45) transparency
- Summary Chart (page 46) transparency, two class sets of photocopies
- Summarizing Paragraphs (page 47) class set of photocopies
- writing template (page 48) class set of photocopies
- rubric (page 8) class set of photocopies

OBJECTIVE

The student will write a one-paragraph summary of a multiple-paragraph passage.

CRITICAL COMPONENTS

- The main idea is stated in the topic sentence.
- The summary contains key points and phrases.
- The closing statement repeats the main idea.

Setting the Stage

Have students play the game "All in One Breath." Ask volunteers to retell familiar stories (e.g., *Goldilocks and the Three Bears*) all in one breath. After several attempts, some students will be successful. Encourage them to reflect on their thinking and to tell you how they decided what to say and what not to say. The idea is that they can only say a few sentences and so they must be short, providing only the most important events—otherwise, they run out of breath! Young students have difficulty summarizing, so this game causes them to think about shortcuts in storytelling and provides you with a lead-in to teaching about summary writing.

Instructional Input

1 Explain to the class that summarizing is a critical skill in school and in daily life. Explain that it's important to be able to say things succinctly or in a short way. Discuss the three steps to summarizing a story or passage as shown here.

> ## Summarizing
> 1. Read the passage.
> 2. Circle (or remember) key words and phrases.
> 3. Write (or say) a sentence about each key word or phrase.

2 Display the Playing the Piano overhead transparency. Read through the passage together. Ask students to think about which words or phrases are the key points as they read.

3 Invite volunteers to share which words or phrases were the key points. Discuss one paragraph at a time. Use an overhead pen to circle each key word or phrase.

4 Display the Summary Chart overhead transparency. Write the main idea of the passage and the key words and phrases you circled. Ask the class to help you write a topic sentence, detail sentences, and a closing statement. Then, write the complete paragraph.

Guided Practice

1 Review the steps to summarizing. Read them aloud, and answer questions.

2 Give each student a Summarizing Paragraphs and a Summary Chart reproducible. Assign students a passage from the Summarizing Paragraphs reproducible, or have them choose their own. Ask students to circle key words and phrases as they read.

3 Have students complete their Summary Chart based on the passage they read. Then, invite volunteers to share which key words and phrases they circled. Have them read aloud their summary.

Independent Practice

1 Invite students to choose a passage from your collection of photocopied nonfiction passages. Have them show you the passage they selected to ensure it is at their reading level.

2 Give each student another Summary Chart reproducible. Encourage students to carefully read their passage, circle key words and phrases, complete their Summary Chart, and write a short summary that includes all the key points.

3 Have students revise and edit their rough draft and then use the rubric to evaluate their writing.

- Have students **publish** their final drafts and illustrations on the writing template reproducible.

- **Create** a class collection of final draft summaries in a book titled *One-Breath Summaries.*

TEACHING HINTS/EXTENSIONS

- Divide the class into small groups, and have each group summarize one passage of a chapter from a social studies textbook. The summaries will provide a nutshell overview of an entire chapter for the class.

- When students summarize an entire chapter or a library book on a related topic of study, have them cut a large foot from construction paper and write their summary on it. Post the feet on a bulletin board so the class can delight in "walking through" a large amount of text in a brief period of time.

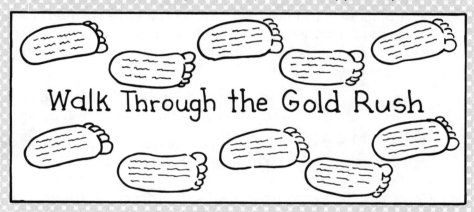

- Students love encyclopedias and often push themselves through difficult text out of sheer curiosity. Encourage them to look up animals in your classroom set of encyclopedias. Invite them to write summaries about and draw a picture of each animal. Bind the summaries and drawings into a class book, or place them in a folder near the encyclopedia set.

- Have students complete one or more of these writing prompts in a journal:
  - ✔ Write a summary of a story in your reading book.
  - ✔ Reread your favorite fairy tale. Write a summary of it.
  - ✔ Write a summary of a class field trip you took.

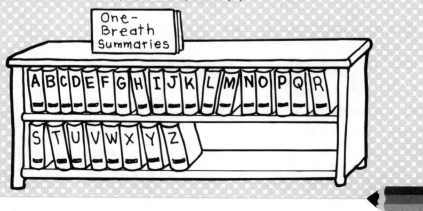

Playing the Piano

Learning to play the piano is fun. It takes a long time to learn to play well. The work is worth it when you learn to play your first song. You should try it. I love to play songs after school.

First, you need to have a piano. Try to have more than a short electronic keyboard. You should have a regular piano with all the keys. There are 88 keys on a piano. It is okay if the piano is not at your house as long as you can play it every day.

Next, you need a good piano teacher. Find a teacher who plays well. Find a teacher who can clearly explain things. Reading music is like reading a book. It takes a while to learn all the symbols. If you have a good teacher, it will be easier and more fun.

After that, learn to read music. That means you can read the notes and rests. The notes are the black dots on the page. Some have stems, and some are circles that are empty inside. The notes tell you which keys to play. Rests look like boxes and squiggly marks. The rests tell you when to pause. When you can read music, you can play almost any song.

Last, you have to practice. If you are in third grade, practice at least 15–20 minutes a day. If you are younger, you can practice about 10–15 minutes a day. If you are older, you might want to practice a half an hour. Some people play an hour or more. If you want to become a good pianist, you have to practice even more.

Playing the piano is fun. You can play for your friends. You can play for your family. You can play at parties. Playing the piano is a rewarding skill.

Steps to Writing Success: Level 2 © 2002 Creative Teaching Press

Summary Chart

Directions: In the left column, list the main idea and key words and phrases (key points) from the passage you read. In the right column, write a topic sentence, a complete sentence for each key point, and a closing statement. Combine these sentences to write a one-paragraph summary at the bottom of the page.

Key Words or Phrases	Sentence Explanations
Main Idea: _____ _____ _____	**Topic Sentence:** _____ _____ _____
Key Points:_____ _____ _____ _____ _____	**Turn each key point into a sentence.** _____ _____ _____ _____
Main Idea (restated):_____ _____ _____	**Closing Statement:** _____ _____ _____

Write a summary. _____
_____
_____
_____
_____

Steps to Writing Success: Level 2 © 2002 Creative Teaching Press

Summarizing Paragraphs

Deviled Eggs

Deviled eggs taste good. They make nice snacks or side dishes. They are healthy. It is interesting to look at the way the colors stay separate. I eat them every day.

To make deviled eggs, boil six eggs. Gently place the eggs in a pan of water. Turn the heat on high. When the water starts to boil, you will see bubbles in the water. Turn the heat down to simmer. Cook the eggs for 15 more minutes.

Next, you need to let the eggs cool. Pour out the hot water. Fill the pan with cold water. Keep running cold water over the eggs until they are cool. Touch the eggs carefully to see if they are cool.

After the eggs cool, you are halfway done. Peel the eggs. If you hold the eggs under cold running water, the shells easily come off. Slice the peeled eggs in half lengthwise. Gently pop out the yokes onto a plate. This is the fun part!

Make the filling next. Smash the yolks with a fork. Then, add ¼ cup (50 mL) of mayonnaise and ¼ teaspoon (1 mL) of fancy mustard. Add a dash of salt and pepper. Mix it all together.

Now you're ready for the last step. Use a table knife to gently fill each egg. Sprinkle the top with paprika. Garnish the eggs with parsley and serve them as a delicious snack or side dish. Enjoy!

Seasons

There are four seasons in a year. They are winter, spring, summer, and fall. Fall is sometimes called autumn. Each season is beautiful and full of surprises. I like them all.

Winter is the coldest season. In the winter, the leaves fall off the trees. We have many thunderstorms. We even have snowstorms. I enjoy winter sports like ice skating and sledding. I also enjoy making snow angels. The cold makes my nose twitch.

Spring brings warmer weather. I can play outside for long periods of time. Spring is the season for new life. I see buds on the trees. I see blooming flowers. I see birds hatching from eggs. In the spring, I plant my own vegetable garden.

In the summer, it gets hot. It gets very, VERY hot. It also gets muggy. I wear shorts and T-shirts and go barefoot when I play. I love to fish and swim in the lake. The vegetable garden grows a lot in the summer. I see tomatoes, cucumbers, bell peppers, and hot peppers ready to pick. The trees are green and full of leaves.

Fall is harvest time. The weather is still hot, but it starts to get cool. The leaves begin to change color. The leaves turn red, orange, and brown, and then they fall to the ground. I pick my pumpkins in the fall. Fall is time to return to school. I have to say good-bye to summer days.

The four seasons are very special. Winter, spring, summer, and fall each have their own beauty and special events. It is difficult to pick a favorite season. I look forward to each one every year!

By

Steps to Writing Success: Level 2 © 2002 Creative Teaching Press

Body Builders

Preparation

Read aloud books about nutrition.

- *The Edible Pyramid: Good Eating Every Day* by Loreen Leedy (Holiday House)
- *Good Enough to Eat: A Kids' Guide to Food and Nutrition* by Lizzy Rockwell (HarperCollins)
- *The Race Against Junk Food* by Anthony Buono and Roy Nemerson (Hcom Inc.)

Gather three pieces of chart paper.

Prepare small pieces of fresh fruit or vegetables on platters with toothpicks and labels that show how to spell the name of each fruit or vegetable. Place the platters on a "sample table" during the Independent Practice activity.

Make copies of these reproducibles.
- Food Guide Pyramid (page 52) transparency, class set of photocopies
- Balanced Meals (page 53) transparency, class set of photocopies
- What's on Your Plate? (page 54) transparency, class set of photocopies
- rubric (page 8) class set of photocopies

OBJECTIVE

The student will write a paragraph that describes a well-balanced meal.

CRITICAL COMPONENTS

- The topic sentence states the name of the meal.

- Detail sentences describe the foods in the meal and how they help the body function.

- The closing statement summarizes the main idea.

Setting the Stage

Discuss nutrition and what students eat each day. Ask what the difference is between a snack and a meal and what students like to eat for a snack when they're hungry. Have students explain why it is important to eat three good meals each day and how their bodies feel if they miss a meal. Explore what good nutrition is by asking volunteers to share what makes a good, healthy meal.

Instructional Input

1 Display the Food Guide Pyramid overhead transparency. Discuss the Food Guide Pyramid and what makes up a day of healthy meals. Explain why students need to eat foods from each group, and discuss how each food group helps the body function.

2 Display the Balanced Meals overhead transparency. Talk about what you ate the preceding day. Sketch the food you ate on the left, and then write the names of the foods on the right.

3 Invite the class to see if you ate nutritious meals by analyzing the food you ate. Tally each type of food you ate on the transparency of the Food Guide Pyramid. Discuss which food groups you got enough servings of and which groups you needed to eat more foods from. Ask the class how you should change your diet to reflect better eating habits. On the Balanced Meals transparency, add pictures and drawings of the foods that would complete a balanced day of eating.

4 Display the What's on Your Plate? overhead transparency. Invite the class to use the information on the Balanced Meals transparency to help you write a paragraph that describes one healthy meal with all the food groups in it. Include information about why different foods are necessary to help your body function.

Guided Practice

1 Give each student a Food Guide Pyramid reproducible. Have students write next to each food group how it helps the body. Name various foods. Have students point to the corresponding food group on their paper and call it out.

2 Place three pieces of chart paper on the board. Label them *Breakfast Foods, Lunch Foods,* and *Dinner Foods.* Invite students to create word banks by sharing and writing nutritious foods for each meal.

3 Give each student a Balanced Meals reproducible. Invite students to draw their meals from the previous day on the left and write the names of the foods on the right. Encourage students to use the word banks to guide them and assist them with spelling. After students record their meals, invite them to write tally marks on their Food Guide Pyramid to show how many servings they ate from each food group.

4 Invite students to add foods to each meal to create balanced meals that provide the correct number of food-group servings throughout the day.

1 Invite students to write a paragraph that describes one meal they recorded on their Balanced Meals reproducible. Remind them to include information about how the different foods help their body function.

2 Invite students to go to the sample table to taste the fruit or vegetables you prepared. Encourage them to add these fruits or vegetables to their balanced meal paragraph.

3 Have students revise and edit their rough draft and then use the rubric to evaluate their writing.

Presentation

• Have students **publish** their final drafts on the What's on Your Plate? reproducible. Have them draw their meal on a paper plate. Or, invite students to write their paragraph on a paper plate and draw the foods included in the meal around the edge of the plate as a border.

• **Invite** students to present their paragraphs to the class. Encourage them to wear healthy food costumes made from construction paper.

• **Display** the final drafts on a bulletin board titled *Healthy Plates* with a border of labels from cans and boxes of food.

TEACHING HINTS/EXTENSIONS

• Set up a "grocery store" in the classroom, complete with food items, a cash drawer, and play bills and coins. Post prices on the food items, and let the buying and selling begin!

• Set up a restaurant learning center. Have students prepare restaurant menus that feature balanced meals and themes, such as Italian food or Mexican food. Remind them to write realistic prices for the food items. Photocopy a set of menus, and invite students to role-play as waiters, waitresses, and customers. Students will practice math skills as they total their customers' bill and use play money to pay for their meals.

• Host a Foods from Around the World Fair in your classroom. Invite parents to prepare sampler plates of food from different countries around the world.

• Have students complete one or more of these writing prompts in a journal:
  ✔ Write a paragraph that describes a nutritious meal for a mountain climber. Remember, the food must be carried in a pack up steep mountains.
  ✔ Write a paragraph that describes a nutritious meal that is perfect for your family to share at home on a Friday night.
  ✔ Write a paragraph that describes a nutritious meal that is perfect for you on a Saturday morning.

Name _____   Date _____

Food Guide Pyramid

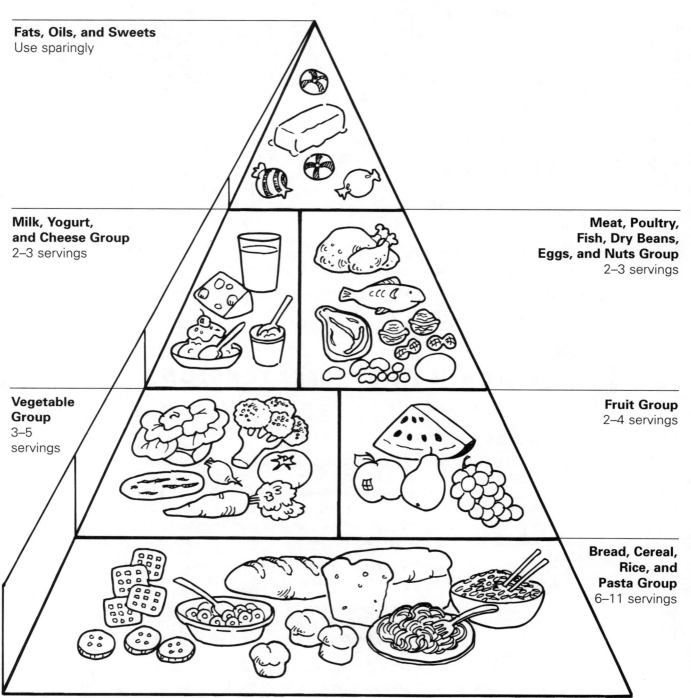

Fats, Oils, and Sweets
Use sparingly

**Milk, Yogurt,
and Cheese Group**
2–3 servings

**Meat, Poultry,
Fish, Dry Beans,
Eggs, and Nuts Group**
2–3 servings

**Vegetable
Group**
3–5
servings

Fruit Group
2–4 servings

**Bread, Cereal,
Rice, and
Pasta Group**
6–11 servings

Name _____ Date _____

Balanced Meals

Breakfast

Lunch

Dinner

What's on Your Plate?

Name _____

Date _____

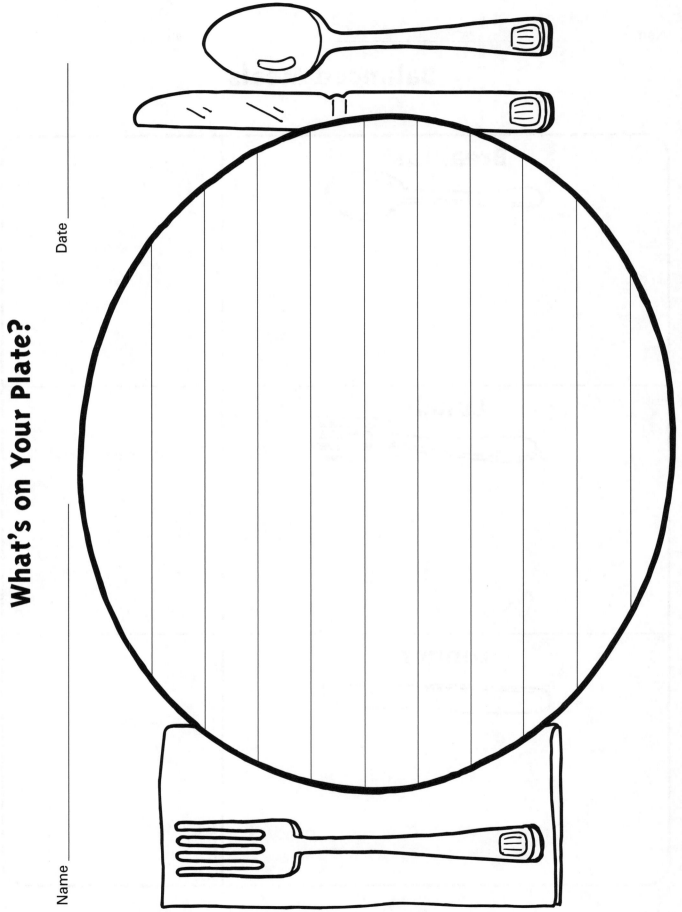

Steps to Writing Success: Level 2 © 2002 Creative Teaching Press

Silly Similes

Preparation

Read aloud books with similes.

- *The Blind Men and the Elephant* by Karen Backstein and Annie Mitra (Scholastic)
- *Eric Carle's Animals Animals* by Eric Carle (Philomel)
- *Quick as a Cricket* by Audrey Wood (Child's Play)

Create a poster of the simile poem "Aussie" in Instructional Input.

Make copies of these reproducibles.
- Simile Puzzles (page 58) one photocopy for every 30 students
- Family Similes (page 59) transparency, class set of photocopies
- writing template (page 60) class set of photocopies
- rubric (page 8) class set of photocopies

Cut apart the Simile Puzzles (page 58).

Setting the Stage

Introduce similes to the class by defining them and giving several examples. Give each student one piece from the Simile Puzzles. Explain that each student has one-half of a "simile sentence" and that students will either have the beginning of a sentence or the last part of a sentence. Have students move around the room until they find the person who has the other half of their simile. After students have paired up with their partner, have them read their simile to the class. Have the class vote on whether they think the simile is correct or not. Ask students to identify what two items are being compared. Collect the pieces and hand them out again. This time, have students try to write a new beginning or ending for their simile.

OBJECTIVE

The student will write two simile poems.

CRITICAL COMPONENTS

- Each simile compares two different things.
- Each simile uses the word *as* or *like*.
- Each poem has at least three comparisons.

Instructional Input

1 Review what similes are. Explain that authors use similes to create vivid pictures in the readers' minds.

2 Display the poster of the simile poem "Aussie," and read it to the class. Emphasize the use of the words *as* and *like* and how they compare two things to each other. Ask students what things were compared in the poem and whether or not they think those were good comparisons.

Aussie

My dog is
as soft as a handful of cotton balls,
as white as freshly fallen snow, and
as cute as a baby's first tooth.

My dog is
jumpy like a yo-yo,
fun like a day at an amusement park, and
happy like a clown smiling all the time.

My dog is
caring like a friend when I'm sad,
whiny like a baby when he's tired, and
as wonderful as a trip in a hot air balloon.

3 Invite students to brainstorm personality and appearance traits that people could have. Write them on the board or chart paper for student reference as they write simile poems.

4 Display the Family Similes overhead transparency. Have students help you write a poem about family members using *as* to compare their personality or appearance to something else. Encourage students to refer to the list of personality and appearance traits they brainstormed. Record their responses on the transparency, and then read aloud the completed poem.

Guided Practice

1 Give each student a Family Similes reproducible. Invite students to work with a partner to write their own similes about family members.

2 Invite students to pick one of their simile sentences to share with the class. Provide feedback as students read their sentences.

Independent Practice

1 Invite students to write simile poems about two members of their family. Ask students to write at least three comparisons for each family member. Encourage them to refer to the poster of the poem "Aussie" as a guide and write their rough draft of each poem on a separate piece of paper. If this is too difficult for some students, invite them to use their sentences from the Family Similes reproducible.

2 Remind students to use a capital letter at the beginning of each sentence, a period at the end of each sentence, and the word *as* or *like* in their comparisons.

3 Have students revise and edit their rough draft and then use the rubric to evaluate their writing.

Presentation

- Have students **publish** their final drafts on the writing template reproducible. Have them draw an illustration next to each simile poem. Remind students to write a title for each poem.

- Have students **create** a book by cutting apart the poems, making construction paper front and back covers, and binding them with string, ribbon, or yarn.

- Invite students to **present** their book to family members at a Family Tea held in the classroom.

TEACHING HINTS/EXTENSIONS

- Show the class a video about animals. (National Geographic's *Really Wild Animals* series has a good collection.) After students observe the behavior of the different animals, have them create a class bulletin board that features similes about the characteristics of the various animals.

- Have students write similes on sentence strips. Ask them to cut each strip after the word *as* or *like* to create a matching game for a learning center. Place each student's strips in a separate envelope.

- Invite students to record on index cards similes that they find as they read books. Have them write their name and the book title on the other side of the card. At the end of the month, award a prize to the student who found the most similes.

- Have students complete one or more of these writing prompts in a journal:
  ✔ Write a simile poem about an insect.
  ✔ Write a paragraph that includes similes about a place you have visited.
  ✔ Close your eyes and think about a season. Write a paragraph that includes similes to describe the season.

Simile Puzzles

The wind blew through my hair like	**a fan.**
His smile is as warm as	**the sun.**
He was as mean as	**a crazy dog.**
She was as shy as	**a mouse.**
Her skin is soft like	**a baby's skin.**
His hair is black like	**the night.**
Her eyes sparkled like	**diamonds.**
His bald head is as shiny as	**a new penny.**
My neighbor is as old as	**a dinosaur.**
The chair is as hard as	**a rock.**
My mom was as busy as	**a beaver.**
My brother is as silly as	**a monkey.**
His eyes are as blue as	**the sky.**
His voice croaked like	**a frog.**
She smelled as sweet as	**a rose.**

Steps to Writing Success: Level 2 © 2002 Creative Teaching Press

Family Similes

Directions: Complete each simile. Write an adjective in the first blank and a noun in the second blank of each sentence.

A mom is as _____

as a _____.

A dad is as _____

as a _____.

A brother is as _____

as a _____.

A sister is as _____

as a _____.

A dog is as _____

as a _____.

A cat is as _____

as a _____.

Steps to Writing Success: Level 2 © 2002 Creative Teaching Press

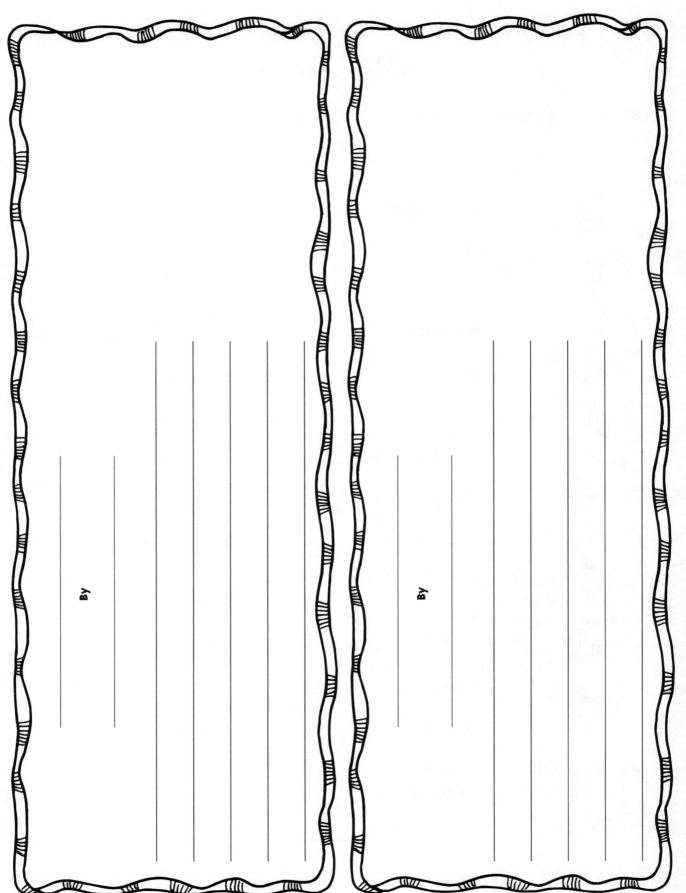

By _____

By _____

Steps to Writing Success: Level 2 © 2002 Creative Teaching Press

Alliteration Acrobatics

Preparation

Read aloud books with alliteration.

- *Animalia* by Graeme Base (Harry N. Abrams)
- *Princess Prunella and the Purple Peanut* by Margaret Atwood (Workman)
- *The Z Was Zapped* by Chris Van Allsburg (Houghton Mifflin)

Make copies of these reproducibles.

- Skit Words (page 63) photocopy
- Alliterative Paragraphs (page 64) transparency
- writing template (page 65) transparency, class set of photocopies
- rubric (page 8) class set of photocopies

Cut apart the Skit Words reproducible (page 63). Place each set of three alliterative words into a separate envelope.

Setting the Stage

Divide the class into ten groups. Give each group an envelope with a set of Skit Words in it. Explain that they will act out three words that begin with the same sound. Invite groups to make up quick pantomimes for their words, tell their alliterative letter, and perform their pantomime. Invite the class to identify the three words.

Instructional Input

1 Explain that the words the groups pantomimed were examples of alliteration because they all had the same sound at the beginning. Give examples of alliteration, and invite students to share their own examples.

2 Display the Alliterative Paragraphs overhead transparency. Read aloud the paragraphs. Invite students to identify and circle the alliterative words.

3 Explain that an alliterative paragraph is one that repeats the same beginning sound in consecutive words or in words in close proximity. Explain that authors use this technique because it makes the paragraph sound pleasing to the ear and adds emphasis to the words.

OBJECTIVE

The student will write three sentences with alliterative words.

CRITICAL COMPONENTS

- Sentences include words with the same initial sound.
- The three sentences tell a short story.
- Complete sentences are written with correct capitalization and punctuation.

Guided Practice

1 Explain that using alliteration sometimes makes writing more interesting to read. For example, explain that *the playful puppy* sounds better than *the frisky puppy*. Ask students to share other alliterative words that can be used to describe the puppy.

2 Choose one of the skits performed by a group in Setting the Stage. Create a word bank of alliterative words that go along with the words pantomimed.

3 Display the writing template overhead transparency. Invite the class to help you write a short alliterative story about the skit that incorporates the additional words from the word bank. Tell students that most, not all, words need to begin with the alliterative sound.

Independent Practice

1 Invite students to work with their group from Setting the Stage to create a word bank of alliterative words that go along with the three words their group pantomimed. Encourage students to use a dictionary to help them brainstorm words.

2 Invite students to write a rough draft of an alliterative story that consists of three sentences. Encourage students to use the word bank they created to supply words for the story.

3 Have students revise and edit their rough draft and then use the rubric to evaluate their writing.

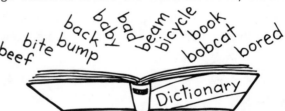

Presentation

● Have students **publish** their final drafts and illustrations on the writing template reproducible.

● **Display** student work on a bulletin board titled *Alphabetical Alliterations.* Add a border with letters of the alphabet.

TEACHING HINTS/EXTENSIONS

● Read aloud a book of tongue twisters such as *Oh Say Can You Say?* by Dr. Seuss (Random House). Invite students to write and publish their own tongue twisters.

● Have students work in small groups to brainstorm alliterative word banks. Have them exchange word banks and use the alliterative words to write paragraphs.

● Invite students to create alliterative collages or posters that tell about some of the things they enjoy. Encourage them to use magazine pictures and words.

● Have students complete one or more of these writing prompts in a journal:
  ✔ Use alliterative words to write about an imaginary creature.
  ✔ Write about a dinosaur. See how many alliterative words you can use to describe it.
  ✔ Write a short alliterative story about a trip.

Skit Words

shake	shoulder	shirt
braid	brush	bracelet
fruit	frown	friend
star	step	stop
dress	drum	draw
space	spider	spin
crocodile	crawl	crab
glue	glove	globe
run	rabbit	race
class	clock	clap

Alliterative Paragraphs

Paragraph #1

Peter promised Papa that he would paint a pretty picture on a pad of paper. Peter planned to practice painting so he could win the prize. He practiced painting a pansy, a purple plum, a plate, a playful puppy, a plant, and a plane.

Paragraph #2

Samantha smiled sweetly while she sat in the sunshine on a Sunday afternoon and sipped a strawberry smoothie. She sat on the sandy shore and saw a ship sailing swiftly over the sea. She smelled the salty air and shivered under the sparkling blue sky.

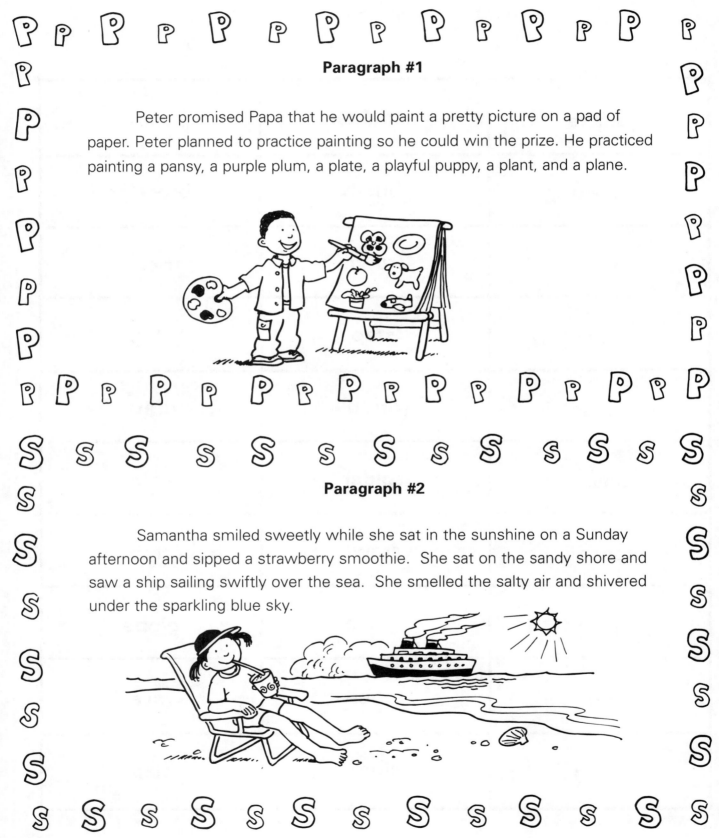

Steps to Writing Success: Level 2 © 2002 Creative Teaching Press

By _____

Countless Colors

Read aloud books about colors.

- *Hello, Red Fox* by Eric Carle (Simon & Schuster)
- *Little Blue and Little Yellow* by Leo Lionni (Mulberry Books)
- *Planting a Rainbow* by Lois Ehlert (Harcourt)

Gather a box of crayons (64 count) for each group of four students.

Make copies of these reproducibles.
- Color Sort Chart (page 69) transparency, one photocopy for every four students
- A Beautiful Bouquet (page 70) transparency
- Birthday Party (page 71) class set of photocopies
- writing template (page 72) class set of photocopies
- rubric (page 8) class set of photocopies

OBJECTIVE

The student will write a descriptive paragraph that includes a variety of color words.

CRITICAL COMPONENTS

- The paragraph focuses on the sense of sight.

- Each sentence includes descriptive, unique color words.

- The paragraph includes a topic sentence and a closing statement.

Setting the Stage

Divide the class into groups of four. Give each group a box of crayons and a copy of the Color Sort Chart. Have groups sort the crayons into the nine categories listed on the chart. Ask groups to write the name of each crayon on their chart. Display the Color Sort Chart overhead transparency. Ask volunteers to share which colors they wrote under each category, and record their responses. Have groups check their charts and correct any errors.

Instructional Input

1 Tell students that they will be writing paragraphs that include visual sensory description related to color. Explain that writing with specific and unique words helps others visualize what the writing is about and what it is describing.

2 Have students close their eyes while you read aloud these two sentences: *I sat on the shore under a bright blue sky and looked out at the ocean's blue waves crested with white foam. I sat on the shore under the sapphire blue sky and looked out at the aquamarine waves crested with ivory foam.*

3 Ask the class if the color word choice affected the way they visualized the scene you described. Invite students to vote for the sentence that was more descriptive and made it easier to visualize the scene. Discuss what the difference was between the two sentences and why students voted as they did. Make sure students understand that the words *blue* and *white* are not as visually descriptive or precise as *sapphire, aquamarine,* and *ivory.*

Guided Practice

1 Explain that writing with predictable color words, such as red, blue, and yellow, can weaken writing, whereas choosing unique and specific color words, such as the names of the crayons, can help the reader visualize the objects being described.

2 Display A Beautiful Bouquet overhead transparency. Read aloud the paragraph with the general color words (shown in parentheses). Reread the paragraph slowly, and ask volunteers to share words from their Color Sort Chart for each blank to make the color descriptions more precise and interesting to read. Invite the class to choose a color word from those shared. Record it in the appropriate blank on the transparency. Reread the paragraph again, and discuss the differences between how it sounded with predictable color words and how it sounded with unique and specific color words.

3 Invite students to discuss the differences between the paragraph as it was read the first time and as it was reread with new words. Ask why the second reading was more powerful.

Independent Practice

1 Explain that students are going to write paragraphs about a birthday party and that they will use visual sensory detail (color words) to describe the decorations and gifts.

2 Ask students to share details about a birthday party. Record their responses on the board.

3 Give each student a Birthday Party reproducible. Review the information students will write about, and then have them complete the reproducible. Have students use the information from each section to write a rough draft paragraph.

4 Have students revise and edit their rough draft and then use the rubric to evaluate their writing.

Presentation

- Have students **publish** their final drafts and illustrations on the writing template reproducible.

- Invite students to **present** their paragraphs. Ask the rest of the class to close their eyes and try to visualize each description.

- **Display** student work on a bulletin board titled *Countless Colors*. Tape crayons with unique names on the bulletin board as a border.

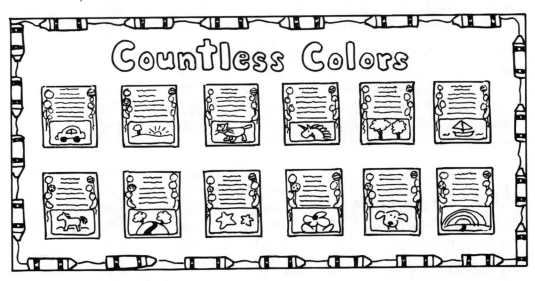

TEACHING HINTS/EXTENSIONS

- Use a color wheel to teach which primary colors can be combined to make secondary colors. Have students sort all their red crayons into a range, from pink to maroon, with all the variety of colors in between to form the complete spectrum of red. Use this same technique with all the other primary colors. Have students use pastel chalk or watercolor paint to draw or paint sunsets.

- Give students a list of objects they can describe in a story such as a pet, a flower, a dinosaur, or stars. Have them work with a partner and find alliterative color words to describe the object such as *lavender lilacs* or *silver stars*.

- Invite students to continue to look for unique color words in books, television shows, or conversations. Cover nine coffee or juice cans with construction paper in various color categories (e.g., blues, reds, browns, greens), and cut blank strips of paper in matching colors. As students discover new color words, have them write the name of the color on one side of the paper strip and their name on the other side. At the end of each month, award the student with the most new color strips with a special privilege.

- Have students complete one or more of these writing prompts in a journal:
  - ✔ List color words to describe the colors you see in a bag of jelly beans. Use these color words to write a paragraph about eating jelly beans.
  - ✔ Close your eyes and imagine fireworks. Write a paragraph about the colors you see.
  - ✔ Write a paragraph that tells about all the colors in a forest.

Color Sort Chart

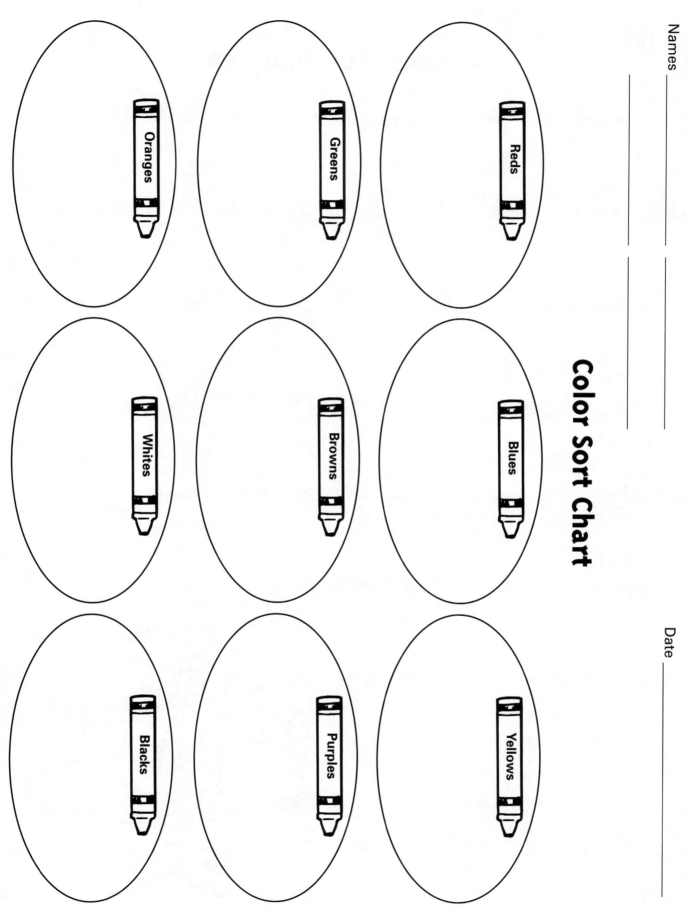

Oranges

Greens

Reds

Whites

Browns

Blues

Blacks

Purples

Yellows

A Beautiful Bouquet

One spring day, I decided to pick a bouquet of flowers for my mom from our flower

garden. First, I found three _____ roses. The tulips were also in bloom,
                                            (red)

so I added two beautiful _____ tulips to the bouquet. Bright
                                      (purple)

_____ daisies caught my eye, and I picked four of them.
              (yellow)

Next, I found three _____ carnations with glossy _____
                              (white)   (green)

stems and leaves to finish the bouquet. I tied a shiny _____ ribbon
                                                                          (blue)

around the lovely flowers and gave them to my mom!

Steps to Writing Success: Level 2 © 2002 Creative Teaching Press

Birthday Party

Opening: Write a topic sentence about a birthday party.

_____

Sentence 2: Describe the balloons and decorations with vivid color words.

Sentence 3: Describe some of the packages and ribbons with vivid color words.

Sentence 4: Describe one of the birthday gifts with vivid color words.

Conclusion: Write a closing statement about the birthday party.

_____

By

_____

_____

_____

_____

_____

_____

_____

_____

_____

_____

Auditory Antics

Preparation

Read aloud books about sounds.

- *Hear That?* by Tama Janowitz (Seastar)
- *Mr. Brown Can Moo! Can You?* by Dr. Seuss (Random House)
- *Polar Bear, Polar Bear, What Do You Hear?* by Bill Martin Jr. (Henry Holt and Company)

Gather chart paper and books about the zoo or animals for the classroom library.

Videotape a short section of a television cartoon. Arrange to have a television and VCR in the classroom.

Make copies of these reproducibles.
- Animal Onomatopoeic Words (page 76) one photocopy for every 24 students
- Onomatopoeic Animal Story (page 77) transparency
- writing template (page 78) class set of photocopies
- rubric (page 8) class set of photocopies

Cut apart the Animal Onomatopoeic Words reproducible (page 76).

Setting the Stage

Play the video clip with the sound muted. Then, discuss with the class the importance of sound in helping us to understand what is happening around us. Ask students to guess what was going on in the video clip. Invite students to guess what was being said. Play the video clip again with the sound on. Discuss the details that were clearer the second time because of the addition of sound. Ask students what sounds they heard, other than dialogue.

OBJECTIVE

The student will

write a paragraph

that includes

onomatopoeic words.

CRITICAL COMPONENTS

- Onomatopoeic words represent a sound with written words.

- The paragraph includes several onomatopoeic words (words that represent sounds, such as *buzz* and *hiss*).

Why can't I hear it?

Instructional Input

1 Tell students that they will be writing descriptive paragraphs that focus on sounds. Explain that sometimes writers use onomatopoeic words—words that sound like the things they represent. Give examples, and have students share examples.

2 Give each student a word from the Animal Onomatopoeic Words reproducible. Have each student read aloud his or her word and identify what animal could have made it. Invite each student to record the word (sound) and animal on chart paper. Emphasize the auditory connection to the written words.

3 Ask students to share other onomatopoeic words with the class. Add them to the chart paper. Leave this word bank posted in the classroom as a reference for students when they write.

```
Onomatopoeia
chirp    → bird
squeal   → pig
quack    → duck
meow     → cat
growl    → lion
hiss     → snake
flutter  → butterfly
```

Guided Practice

1 Explain that using onomatopoetic words makes writing more vivid and interesting to the reader. Ask students which of the following two statements is more interesting: *The lamp fell to the ground and broke* or *Crash! The lamp fell to the ground and broke with a thud.* Point out that replacing dull words with onomatopoeic words made the writing stronger and easier to visualize the event being described.

2 Display the Onomatopoeic Animal Story overhead transparency. Read it aloud with the blanks. Reread it, but stop at each blank and ask a volunteer to suggest a word from the onomatopoetic word bank. If students think of additional words, add them to the chart paper.

3 Ask the whole class to read aloud the completed story. Assign onomatopoeic words from the story blanks to volunteers. Invite the class to read the story again, and have the volunteers make the sounds of the onomatopoeic words.

Independent Practice

1 Have students write a story that includes onomatopoeia. Invite them to use the Onomatopoeic Animal Story reproducible or write their own original story.

2 Give each student either an Onomatopoeic Animal Story reproducible or lined paper. Encourage students to use words from the word bank in their story, and encourage them to add words to the chart paper as they think of new ones. Invite students to browse through zoo and animal books in the classroom library for ideas.

3 Have students revise and edit their rough draft and then use the rubric to evaluate their writing.

Presentation

- Have students **publish** their final drafts on the writing template reproducible. Invite them to draw an illustration on a separate piece of paper.

- Have students **present** their stories. Invite them to ask classmates to help them make onomatopoeic sounds.

- **Bind** the stories into a class book titled *Yippee! Sound Stories.*

TEACHING HINTS/EXTENSIONS

- Play nature cassettes or videotapes of the sounds of animals in the jungle while students are writing.

- Plan a field trip to the zoo. If the field trip is *before* the writing lesson, encourage students to listen for unusual sounds they could incorporate in their writing. If the field trip is *after* the writing lesson, have students add new onomatopoeic words to the word bank.

- Invite students to bring in animal pictures and use them to create a class mural on a long sheet of butcher paper. Have students add a speech bubble with the corresponding onomatopoetic sound next to each animal.

- Have students complete one or more of these writing prompts in a journal:
    - ✔ Use onomatopoeia to write a paragraph about the sounds at the airport.
    - ✔ Write a paragraph about a vacation trip on a train. Describe the sounds you hear using onomatopoeia.
    - ✔ Write a paragraph about a loud and intense thunderstorm. Use onomatopoeic words in your description.

Animal Onomatopoeic Words

arf	meow
bleat	mew
bray	moo
bow-wow	neigh
caw	oink
cheep	purr
chirp	quack
cluck	snarl
growl	snort
flutter	squeak
hiss	squeal
howl	tweet

Steps to Writing Success: Level 2 © 2002 Creative Teaching Press

Name _____ Date _____

Onomatopoeic Animal Story

Last week, I went to one of my favorite places, the zoo. The first animal I wanted

to see was the _____ that says, "_____."

Across the path was the _____ cage, and they were screaming,

"_____!" This upset the _____ , and it began to

loudly cry "_____." Suddenly, a _____ escaped

from its cage screeching, "_____." Luckily, I had some

_____ to feed the _____ and the zookeeper was

able to lead it safely back to its cage.

Steps to Writing Success: Level 2 © 2002 Creative Teaching Press

_____

By

_____

Steps to Writing Success: Level 2 © 2002 Creative Teaching Press

Food Festival

Preparation

Read aloud books about smelling and tasting.

- *Eating and Tasting* by Henry Pluckrose (Raintree Steck-Vaughn)
- *Snuffles* by Joan Anson-Weber (Cherokee)
- *You Can't Smell a Flower with Your Ear: All About Your 5 Senses* by Joanna Cole (Price Stern Sloan)

Gather two pieces of chart paper.

Label six plastic film canisters A–F; saturate six cotton balls with a variety of scents, such as lemon juice, vinegar, perfume, or extract oils such as mint, vanilla, or cinnamon; place one cotton ball in each canister; and fill six small paper bags with enough food, such as popcorn, chocolate, marshmallows, and carrots, for each student to taste.

Make copies of these reproducibles.
- Mystery (page 82) six photocopies
- Favorite Food Festival (page 83) transparency, class set of photocopies
- writing template (page 84) class set of photocopies
- rubric (page 8) class set of photocopies

Setting the Stage

Divide the class into six groups. Give each group a Mystery reproducible and a plastic film canister with a cotton ball. Tell each student to smell the cotton ball and try to identify the smell. Have groups trade canisters at least two times, smell the cotton balls, and complete the top of their reproducible. Then, give each group one small paper bag, and have each student taste the food inside. Ask groups to trade bags and complete the bottom of their reproducible. Encourage volunteers to share what they wrote for each smell and taste.

OBJECTIVE

The student will use sensory detail to write a paragraph that describes the senses of smell and taste.

CRITICAL COMPONENTS

- Sentences descriptively characterize the smell of favorite foods.

- Sentences descriptively characterize the taste of favorite foods.

- The paragraph has a topic sentence and a closing statement.

Instructional Input

1 Tell the class that they will be writing a paragraph that focuses on the senses of smell and taste. Explain that writers use sensory words to describe how a food smells and tastes to strengthen their writing and make it more appealing to readers. Ask students which of the following sentences gives them a better sensory image: *The girl ate an apple* or *The girl ate a crisp, juicy apple.* Have students explain how the sentences are different and why one is more descriptive.

2 Ask students to think of adjectives that describe the way foods smell and taste. Record their responses on chart paper. Leave this word bank posted in the classroom as a reference for students when they write.

3 Draw a three-column chart on another piece of chart paper, and write the headings *Food, Smell,* and *Taste*. Ask students what foods most people eat on Thanksgiving Day (e.g., cranberry sauce, apple pie). Record their responses under "Food."

4 Tell students to imagine that they just walked into the kitchen and can smell all the wonderful scents that go along with Thanksgiving dinner. For each food on the chart, invite students to name words that describe its smell (e.g., sweet) and taste (e.g., yummy). Record their responses on the chart.

Guided Practice

1 Explain that when students write a sensory description, they should use words that help the reader remember and experience the taste and smell of the foods they are describing.

2 Display the Favorite Food Festival overhead transparency. Invite students to help you fill in the blanks. Encourage students to use the word bank and add adjectives that describe smells and tastes as they think of them. Read aloud the completed sentences.

3 Give each student a Favorite Food Festival reproducible. Invite students to complete the four paragraphs and then read them to a partner.

Independent Practice

1 Ask students to think about their favorite meal and sketch all the foods in it.

2 Invite students to write a paragraph that describes the smell and taste of each food in their favorite meal. Emphasize the importance of choosing sensory words that characterize the smells and tastes of their favorite foods. Encourage students to use the word bank of adjectives and write additional words on the chart paper as they think of them.

3 Have students revise and edit their rough draft and then use the rubric to evaluate their writing.

Presentation

- Have students **publish** their final drafts on the writing template reproducible. Invite students to draw an illustration on a separate piece of paper.

- Have students **create** models of their meals on paper plates. Have them use clay or construction paper to make their models.

- **Display** the paragraphs and models for parents at a "Food Festival." Invite students to bring in samples of their meal for guests to smell and taste.

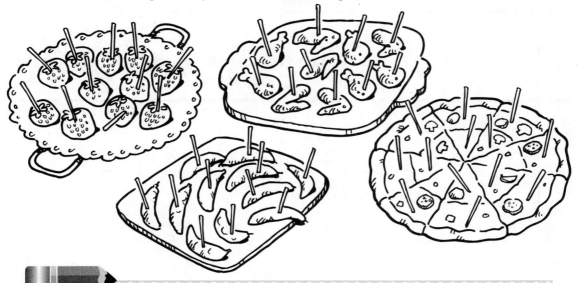

TEACHING HINTS/EXTENSIONS

- Invite students to compile lists of class favorites in each of the following categories: dessert, drinks, breakfast, and fruit. Tally the results, and draw bar graphs and pie graphs to display the results.

- Encourage students to write riddles about their favorite foods and read them in front of the class. For example, a student might write *I am orange. I am long and thin. I wear a green "hat." What am I?* (carrot) Have the class try to answer each riddle.

- Invite students to create Food Guide Pyramid collages with pictures of their favorite foods from each food group.

- Have students complete one or more of these writing prompts in a journal:
    - ✔ Write a sensory detail paragraph about your favorite food. Describe what it smells and tastes like.
    - ✔ Write a paragraph that describes some of your favorite smells.
    - ✔ Imagine you just got hired as an ice-cream taster for the summer. Tell about the flavors you have tasted.

Names _____   Date _____

_____

  **Mystery**

Smells

Mystery Can	What is it?	List two descriptive words.	How did the smell make you feel?
A		1. 2.	
B		1. 2.	
C		1. 2.	
D		1. 2.	
E		1. 2.	
F		1. 2.	

Tastes

Food	Descriptive Word	Descriptive Word

Steps to Writing Success: Level 2 © 2002 Creative Teaching Press

Favorite Food Festival

My favorite breakfast food is _____.

It smells _____. It tastes

_____ and _____.

It reminds me of _____.

My favorite drink is _____.

It smells _____. It tastes

_____ and _____.

It reminds me of _____.

My favorite fruit is _____.

It smells _____. It tastes

_____ and _____.

It reminds me of _____.

My favorite dessert is _____.

It smells _____. It tastes

_____ and _____.

It reminds me of _____.

By

Steps to Writing Success: Level 2 © 2002 Creative Teaching Press

Kinesthetic Clues

Preparation

Read aloud books about the sense of touch.

- *Feeling Things* by Allen Fowler (Children's Press)
- *King Midas and the Golden Touch* by Charlotte Craft (Morrow Junior)
- *The Sweet Touch* by Lorna Balien (Humbug Books)

Gather a clipboard for every pair of students, chart paper, and a large bag made of cloth (so students can't see what's inside).

Invite each student to bring one interesting item from home for the "mystery bag."

Make copies of these reproducibles.
- Investigative Report (page 88) transparency, class set of photocopies
- Investigation Data (page 89) one photocopy for every two students
- writing template (page 90) class set of photocopies
- rubric (page 8) class set of photocopies

OBJECTIVE

The student will use sensory detail words to write an investigative report about the sense of touch.

CRITICAL COMPONENTS

- Paragraphs include several words that relate to the sense of touch.

- Paragraphs have a topic sentence and a closing statement.

Setting the Stage

Collect students' items for the mystery bag as they enter the classroom in the morning. Encourage students who forgot an item to choose one from the classroom. Show the mystery bag to the class, and explain that you will call students up to the bag one at a time to reach in, feel one item, and try to identify what it is based entirely on how it feels. Encourage students to describe to the class how the item feels. Invite them to guess what it is and then take the item out of the bag to see if their guess was correct.

Instructional Input

1 Tell students that they will act as "detectives" to solve a "mystery" on the school playground and then write a paragraph that includes sensory detail words that relate to the sense of touch. Discuss the job of a detective, and remind students that detectives must look at all the clues very carefully so they can figure out the mystery.

2 Ask students to think of words that describe how something feels. Record their responses on chart paper. Leave this word bank posted in the classroom as a reference for students when they write.

3 Display the Investigative Report overhead transparency. Invite the class to read the story aloud together (with the blanks). Tell students that the blank spaces need to be filled in with objects that can be touched and words that tell how the objects feel. Invite volunteers to write objects and sensory words in the blanks. Encourage them to use the word bank if they need ideas.

Guided Practice

1 Divide the class into pairs, and take students outside to the playground. Give each pair an Investigation Data reproducible and a clipboard.

2 Ask partners to touch five different objects on the playground, record them under "Item" on their data sheet, and write a descriptive word or words that explain how each object feels.

3 Return to the classroom, and have partners compare the words and objects on their data sheet with other partners.

4 Give each student an Investigative Report reproducible. Tell students to use some of the sensory detail words and objects they recorded on their data sheet to fill in the blanks. Invite volunteers to share their story with the class.

Independent Practice

1 Invite students to write their own original detective story about a playground mystery such as a lost shoe or a missing lunchbox. Tell them to use sensory detail words to describe the objects they touch. Remind students to refer to the word bank and their data sheet to guide them.

2 Have students revise and edit their rough draft and then use the rubric to evaluate their writing.

Presentation

- Have students **publish** their final drafts on the writing template reproducible. Invite students to draw an illustration on a separate piece of paper.

- **Invite** students to present their stories. Encourage them to wear a detective hat and hold props related to their mysteries.

- **Display** student work on a bulletin board titled *Natural Investigators.*

TEACHING HINTS/EXTENSIONS

- Invite students to write riddles that include the sense of touch. For example, the clues could be *I am smooth and slippery. I am usually wet because I live in the water. I have eight legs. What am I?* (octopus)

- Give a piece of lined paper to the student at the beginning of each row or table group, and have the students write a sentence at the top of the page to begin a "sensory detail story." Tell students to include sensory detail words in every sentence they write. Then, have students fold the paper over the first sentence and, a bit lower on the page, write the first two or three words of the second sentence. Ask students to pass the paper to the next person, and have that student finish the second sentence, fold the paper, and add two or three words to start the third sentence. Continue the procedure until each paper is completely folded. Read aloud each story.

- Build on the students' new familiarity with the sense of touch by inviting them to further investigate how the blind use the sense of touch to read Braille. Bring samples of Braille books for students to explore. Invite a speaker to talk about blind education and the use of the Braille reading system. Read stories about Helen Keller, Stevie Wonder, and other famous blind individuals who have made significant contributions to society despite being unable to see.

- Have students complete one or more of these writing prompts in a journal:
  - ✔ Write a paragraph that describes what you would feel at a reptile petting zoo.
  - ✔ Write a paragraph about what it feels like to walk barefoot at the beach.
  - ✔ Write a sensory detail paragraph about exploring a dark, dusty cave.

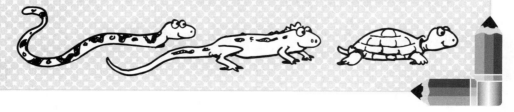

Investigative Report

The Case of the Sticky Juice Trail

Hi! I'm Detective _____.

I just received an important case. My teacher,

_____, of _____

School, told me that every morning there is a sticky juice trail

throughout the playground. My crime-solving partner,

_____, and I began our investigation. We

walked around the playground trying to gather as many clues as

possible. First, we felt the _____ of the

_____ , which felt _____.

Then, we followed the trail to the _____,

which felt very _____. By this time, my

partner and I were very confused. We kept going until we came to

the _____ and noticed sticky fingerprints

all over it! We knew we were close to solving the case! Our one

last area to investigate was the _____. It

felt _____ and _____.

Finally, we realized who had left the juice trail! It was

_____!

Steps to Writing Success: Level 2 © 2002 Creative Teaching Press

Names _____   Date _____

_____

Investigation Data

Item	What Does It Feel Like?

By

_____

_____

_____

_____

_____

_____

_____

_____

_____

_____

_____

Steps to Writing Success: Level 2 © 2002 Creative Teaching Press

Fantastic Feelings

Read aloud poems about emotions.

Preparation

- *The Random House Book of Poetry for Children* by Jack Prelutsky (Random House)
- *Rose, Where Did You Get That Red?: Teaching Great Poetry to Children* by Kenneth Koch (Vintage Books)
- *Where the Sidewalk Ends* by Shel Silverstein (HarperCollins)

Gather a piece of white construction paper and four craft sticks for each student.

Make copies of these reproducibles.
- Story about Feelings (page 94) transparency
- Loneliness is . . . (page 95) transparency
- writing template (page 96) two or three transparencies, class set of photocopies
- rubric (page 8) class set of photocopies

Setting the Stage

Discuss what emotions are. Have students share examples of when they feel certain emotions and how they act when they feel them. Record emotions on the board or chart paper. Give each student a piece of white construction paper and four craft sticks. Invite students to fold the paper in fourths and draw in each section a face that shows happiness, sadness, fear, and surprise. Have students cut out the faces and glue each one to a separate craft stick. Display the Story about Feelings overhead transparency. Tell students that you are going to read a story that will have situations that may be happy, sad, frightening, or surprising. Encourage students to hold up the stick with the facial expression that depicts each emotion as it occurs in the story. Discuss the emotions in the story and how students knew what the main character was feeling.

OBJECTIVE

The student will write a poem that describes an emotion.

CRITICAL COMPONENTS

- Sentences begin with the same emotion (e.g., *Happiness is, Sadness is*).

- Sentences describe experiences that relate to the specific emotion.

Instructional Input

1 Tell students that they will be writing poems that illustrate an emotion based on experiences that they have heard about, read about, or experienced personally. Explain that good authors include specific, detailed examples to help the reader experience the emotion they are describing.

2 Display the Loneliness is . . . overhead transparency. Invite the class to read it aloud. Ask students if they were able to visualize the situations described in the poem and why they were able to do so.

3 Invite students to volunteer other experiences they could add to the poem to further describe loneliness. Record their responses on the transparency.

Guided Practice

1 Display a writing template overhead transparency. Write *Sadness* in each blank before the word "is."

2 Invite the class to work together to write a "definition poem" about sadness. Divide the class into pairs, and have each pair write two sentences that begin with *Sadness is*.

3 Ask partners to choose one of their sentences to share with the class. Record the sentences on several transparencies. Read the completed poem together as a class.

Independent Practice

1 Invite students to choose one of the other emotions described in Story about Feelings (i.e., happiness, surprise, fear) or an emotion the class brainstormed in Setting the Stage and write their own definition poem about it. Remind students to choose specific experiences that will help the reader visualize and feel the emotion they are describing.

2 Encourage students to write at least six sentences for their poem. Remind them to write a title and begin each sentence the same way (e.g., *Fear is, Happiness is*).

3 Have students revise and edit their rough draft and then use the rubric to evaluate their writing.

Presentation

- Have students **publish** their final drafts on the writing template reproducible. (Students will need more than one if they write more than six sentences.)

- Invite students to **create** illustrations on separate pieces of paper to depict each sentence in their poem and write each sentence above or below the corresponding picture.

- Invite students to **present** their poem and have classmates hold up the illustration for each sentence.

- Encourage students to **make** front and back covers and combine their poem and illustrations to create their own book.

TEACHING HINTS/EXTENSIONS

- Invite students to choose an emotion and create a visual poster that illustrates what that emotion looks like. Encourage them to cut out magazine pictures of people's facial expressions and landscapes that visually demonstrate the emotion, such as a peaceful lake or a lightning storm. Have them glue their pictures on a piece of colored construction paper that relates to that emotion, such as red for anger.

- Ask students to bring in a photograph of themselves with a facial expression that illustrates one of the emotions discussed in class. Give students time to tell about the experience that led them to feel that emotion. Have students write a paragraph about the experience. Create a class photo gallery by placing each student's photo next to his or her story.

- Collect a variety of wordless picture books, such as *Frog Goes to Dinner* by Mercer Mayer (Dial Books), *Good Dog, Carl* by Alexandra Day (Simon & Schuster), and *The Hunter and the Animals* by Tomie dePaola (Holiday House). Ask students to choose a partner, read a story together, and identify the emotions of the characters in the story. Have them write text to accompany every picture in the book. Remind them to focus on the feelings and emotions of the characters.

- Have students complete one or more of these writing prompts in a journal:
  ✔ Write a definition poem about friendship or a good friend.
  ✔ Write a definition poem titled *Courage is . . .*
  ✔ Think about Martin Luther King Jr. and write a poem titled *Freedom is . . .*

Story about Feelings

Kaylee went shopping at the grocery store with her mom. She liked to help pick out the groceries. First, they walked down the produce aisle. Kaylee frowned as she saw her mom pick out some broccoli. She grabbed her mom's hand and led her over to the strawberries. "Can we buy some of these?" she asked. Just then, Kaylee was startled to see her teacher across the aisle. "Hi, Mrs. Jones," Kaylee said shyly.

The next aisle was Kaylee's favorite—the cereal and toy aisle. While her mom selected her favorite cereal, Kaylee looked at the toys. She found a super ball and started bouncing it. It bounced too hard and hit a lady in the head. The lady yelled at Kaylee and made her cry. "I think we better go home now," Kaylee's mom said.

On the way out of the store, Kaylee asked if she could ride the little merry-go-round. Her mom said, "I don't have any quarters, but you can sit on one of the horses if you'd like." Kaylee climbed up and barely sat down when the horse started moving. Kaylee screamed at first, but then she smiled and held on for the remainder of the ride.

Loneliness is . . .

Loneliness is being chosen last for soccer.

Loneliness is when your best friend moves away.

Loneliness is eating lunch by yourself.

Loneliness is not being invited to your classmate's birthday party.

Loneliness is the first day at a new school.

Loneliness is getting separated from your family at the mall.

Loneliness is _____

_____

_____ .

Loneliness is _____

_____

_____ .

_____

By

_____

_____ is _____

_____

_____ is _____

_____

_____ is _____

_____

_____ is _____

_____

_____ is _____

_____

_____ is _____

_____

Steps to Writing Success: Level 2 © 2002 Creative Teaching Press

Postcard Dreams

Preparation

Read aloud books with descriptions of various settings.

- *Letters from Felix: A Little Rabbit on a World Tour* by Annette Langen (Abbeville Press)
- *Miss Rumphius* by Barbara Cooney (Viking)
- *The Town Mouse and the Country Mouse* by Jan Brett (Putnam)

Gather chart paper.

Collect for each student a postcard or magazine picture of a place.

Make copies of these reproducibles.
- Passage Comparison (page 100) transparency
- The Zoo (page 101) transparency
- writing template (page 102) one photocopy for every two students
- rubric (page 8) transparency, class set of photocopies

Cut each writing template reproducible in half.

OBJECTIVE

The student will write on a postcard a paragraph that describes a setting.

CRITICAL COMPONENTS

- The topic sentence includes the name of the setting.

- Detail sentences include sensory details that describe the setting.

- The paragraph includes a closing statement that restates the main idea.

Setting the Stage

Explain that every story or book has a setting— the place where the story occurs. Ask what the setting was in familiar stories such as *Little Red Riding Hood* (woods and grandma's house). Place several of the books you read during the preceding week on the chalkboard or whiteboard ledge. Ask students to describe each setting. Write their responses above each book. Show the postcards you collected, and invite each student to choose one. Have students share with a partner what they find attractive about their postcard's setting. Tell students that an oral or a written description of the setting could help them decide whether or not they would go there if they did not have a picture of it. Invite several volunteers to describe their setting while students close their eyes to visualize it. Have students hold on to their postcard for Independent Practice.

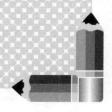

Instructional Input

1 Ask students why settings are an important part of a story. Explain that settings must be described in detail so that the reader can imagine what the writer has in mind. Emphasize that a story wouldn't be complete and may not work without a proper setting. For example, ask students how *Charlotte's Web* by E. B. White (HarperCollins) would change if the setting were in an airplane instead of on a farm.

2 Display the Passage Comparison overhead transparency. Cover the illustrations on the bottom of the transparency. Read aloud Passage #1. Then, read aloud Passage #2. Invite students to explain which passage is more interesting and why.

3 Ask students which passage they could visualize easily in their head. Discuss why the second passage was effective. Underline the name of the setting in both the topic and closing sentences of the first paragraph, and circle or draw a box around all the words that students can visualize. Reveal the illustrations, and discuss whether the visual pictures in students' heads matched the illustrations.

Guided Practice

1 Display The Zoo overhead transparency. Ask students what they see in the illustration. Read aloud the words, and discuss zoos with the class. Record details from the discussion on chart paper.

2 Ask students to close their eyes and imagine a time they visited a zoo or what it would be like if they did. Have each student share one word about the experience (e.g., fun, smelly, elephant), and add it to the chart paper.

3 Invite the class to help you write a paragraph that describes the setting of the zoo and can be easily visualized by the reader. Encourage students to use words listed on the chart paper in addition to the ones in the illustration. Start with a topic sentence that names the setting. Write at least three sentences that describe the setting (include sensory details) and a closing statement that restates the main idea of the paragraph.

4 Display the rubric overhead transparency. Have students help you revise and edit the paragraph.

Independent Practice

1 Have students take out their postcard. Ask them to imagine their postcard location as a story setting. Invite students to list on a piece of paper words that describe their setting. Encourage them to share their words with a classmate and help each other write more words. Tell students to write a paragraph about their setting.

2 Have students revise and edit their rough draft and then use the rubric to evaluate their writing.

● Have students **publish** their paragraphs on the writing template reproducible.

● **Display** each postcard next to its corresponding paragraph on a bulletin board titled *Postcard Dreams*.

TEACHING HINTS/EXTENSIONS

● Have students cut out magazine pictures of potential story settings. Then, have them write paragraphs that describe these settings.

● Collect setting paragraphs from the previous extension, and keep them in the writing center. Have students use them as story starters.

● Invite students to collect interesting setting descriptions as they read during Sustained Silent Reading time. Have them record the passages in their reading journals. During a designated sharing time, have students share the settings they found.

● Have students complete one or more of these writing prompts in a journal:
  ✔ Write a paragraph that describes the setting of a story that takes place in a submarine.
  ✔ Write a paragraph that describes the setting of a story that takes place in an imaginary world.
  ✔ Write a paragraph that describes the setting of a story that takes place inside a squirrel's nest deep in a wooded forest.

Passage Comparison

Passage #1

It was morning on the farm. Henrietta was very grumpy this morning. She was not cooperating. I got really mad and kicked the milk bucket.

Passage #2

As the sun rose over the farm, the rooster crowed atop the old red barn. Surrounding green meadows glistened with dew. Crows perched on the wood fence. It was a cool summer morning. I was happy to be on Grandpa's farm once again.

Inside the barn, it smelled like fresh hay. Henrietta, the milking cow, lazily stood in her stall as a fly buzzed overhead. I opened the door and led her outside.

I sat down on the tiny wood stool and tried to milk her, but she kicked her feet and swished her tail at me. I got so mad I kicked the milk bucket over.

Teacher Note: Do not reveal the scenes below until the class has discussed the passages.

Steps to Writing Success: Level 2 © 2002 Creative Teaching Press

The Zoo

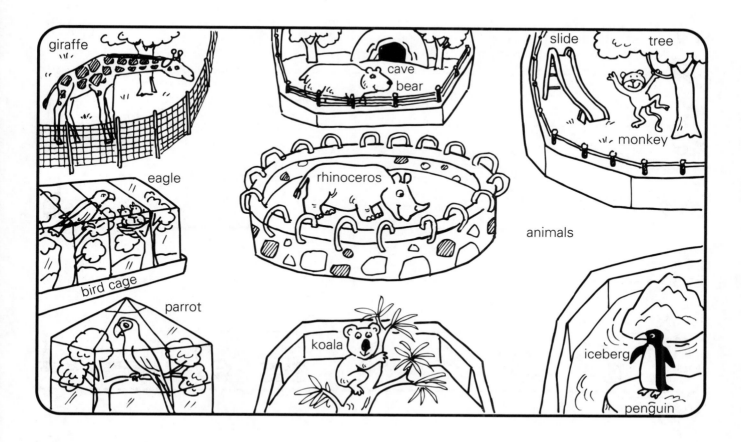

_____

_____

_____

_____

_____

_____

_____

Steps to Writing Success: Level 2 © 2002 Creative Teaching Press

By _____

_____

_____

_____

_____

_____

- -

By _____

_____

_____

_____

_____

_____

Friendship Circle

Read aloud books with strong descriptions of characters.

- *Amazing Grace* by Mary Hoffman (Dial Books)
- *King Bob's New Clothes* by Dom DeLuise (Aladdin)
- *Mrs. Katz and Tush* by Patricia Polacco (Yearling Books)

Create a toy microphone by wrapping a sugar cone with foil and taping a ball of foil on top.

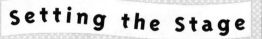

Make copies of these reproducibles.
- Friendship Circle (page 106) transparency, 1½ class sets of photocopies
- Closer Look (page 107) transparency, one photocopy for every two students
- Meet My Friend (page 108) transparency, class set of photocopies
- rubric (page 8) transparency, class set of photocopies

Setting the Stage

Write the following questions on the board: *What is your friend's name? What kind of personality does he or she have? What kinds of special skills does he or she have? How and when did you meet? What do you like to do together?* Use the toy microphone to interview several volunteers about a special friend. Then, invite a student to use the toy microphone to interview you. Describe a character from a book you have been reading, but keep the name a secret. Invite the class to identify the mystery character. Repeat this activity with several characters.

OBJECTIVE

The student will write a paragraph that describes a character.

CRITICAL COMPONENTS

- The paragraph includes a topic sentence with the character's name.

- The paragraph includes details about the character's personality and special skills.

- The paragraph includes a closing statement with a final thought about the character.

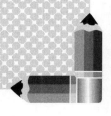

Instructional Input

1 Ask students to help you brainstorm personality characteristics of friends, special skills friends may have, places to meet new friends, and things they like to do with friends. Record their responses on the board or chart paper.

2 Display the Friendship Circle overhead transparency. Discuss characters the class recently read about. Ask the class to choose one character to be their friend. Have students imagine that they too were a character in the story, and ask them to help you fill in the information for the transparency.

3 Display the Closer Look overhead transparency. Write about the character described on the Friendship Circle transparency. Read aloud the completed transparency. Ask students if there is any other information that needs to be added.

4 Display the Meet My Friend overhead transparency. Use the information from the Closer Look transparency to write a paragraph about the character. Display the rubric overhead transparency, and have students help you revise and edit the paragraph.

Guided Practice

1 Invite students to work with a partner to write a description of a character. Give each pair of students a Friendship Circle and a Closer Look reproducible. Encourage partners to choose a character in a book they have both read and imagine that they too are characters in the story.

2 Ask partners to complete the two reproducibles and then share with the class the information they recorded on their Closer Look reproducible. Invite the class to suggest additional information that partners could add.

Independent Practice

1 Give each student a Friendship Circle reproducible. Invite students to make up a character and record information about him or her. Tell students to imagine that they met this character in a story.

2 Have students write a rough draft paragraph that describes their character. If students need more structure to write this paragraph, invite them to complete another copy of the Closer Look reproducible about their character.

3 Have students revise and edit their rough draft and then use the rubric to evaluate their writing.

● Have students **publish** their final drafts and illustrations on the Meet My Friend reproducible.

● **Create** a "character quilt" by hole-punching each side of each Meet My Friend reproducible and connecting the papers with yarn.

● **Display** the character quilt on a classroom wall or in the school hallway or front office.

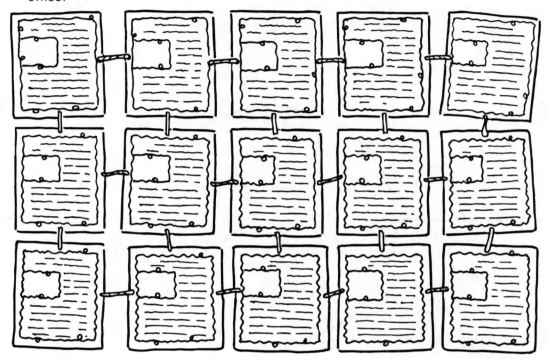

TEACHING HINTS/EXTENSIONS

● Invite students to mold busts of their characters with clay, and display them near the character quilt.

● Use students' final drafts as story starters. Place the character quilt in a writing center, and invite students to write stories about characters their classmates created or weave several characters from the character quilt into a humorous adventure.

● Invite students to write paragraphs about special friends, and post them in a circle on a bulletin board titled *Friendship Circle*.

● Have students complete one or more of these writing prompts in a journal:
  ✔ Write a paragraph about a character that is from another country.
  ✔ Write a description of a character that lives in the ocean.
  ✔ Describe a character that gets into mischief.

Friendship Circle

2. I would describe my friend's personality as . . .

3. His or her special skills are . . .

1. My friend's name is

_____

4. We met . . .

5. We like to . . .

Steps to Writing Success: Level 2 © 2002 Creative Teaching Press

Name _____   Date _____

Closer Look

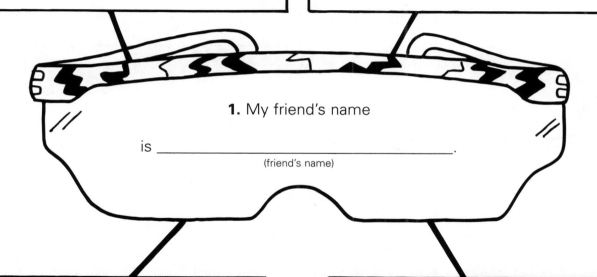

2. _____ is a wonderful
(friend's name)

friend because _____
(personality)

_____

_____ .

3. _____
(friend's name)

has some special skills, including

_____

(special skills)

_____

_____ .

1. My friend's name

is _____ .
(friend's name)

4. We met _____
(where and when)

_____

_____

_____

_____ .

5. We like to _____
(favorite activities)

_____

_____

_____

_____ .

Meet My Friend

By _____

_____

_____

_____

_____

_____

_____

_____

_____

_____

_____

_____

_____

_____

Mirror, Mirror

Preparation

Read aloud short auto-biographical stories.

- *The Art Lesson* by Tomie dePaola (Putnam)
- *Author: A True Story* by Helen Lester (Houghton Mifflin)
- *The Keeping Quilt* by Patricia Polacco (Simon & Schuster)

Gather three objects that represent your life.

Invite each student to bring three objects that represent his or her life.

Make copies of these reproducibles.
- Autobiographical Brainstorm (page 112) transparency, two class sets of photocopies
- writing template (page 113) transparency, class set of photocopies
- rubric (page 8) class set of photocopies

Setting the Stage

Share the three objects that represent your life. Talk about these objects with your students. Explain why you brought them and how they represent your life (e.g., *The teacup represents that I love to drink tea with my friends when we talk*). Invite students to share the three objects that represent their lives. (You may want to spread this activity out over a couple of days or have students only share one item.)

OBJECTIVE

The student will write an autobio-graphical paragraph that includes at least three details about his or her life.

CRITICAL COMPONENTS

- The paragraph includes a topic sentence with the author's name.

- The paragraph includes at least three details about the author's life.

- The paragraph includes a closing statement with a final thought about the author's life.

Instructional Input

1 Discuss what an autobiography is. Explain that it is a book that a person writes about his or her life. Invite students to share the titles of some of the autobiographies you read during the preceding week. Ask students to share what each book was about and what made it an autobiography.

2 Tell students that they are going to write an autobiographical paragraph about themselves and the three items they brought to school.

3 Display the Autobiographical Brainstorm overhead transparency. Fill in the information based on yourself and your objects.

4 Display the writing template overhead transparency. Invite students to help you write your autobiographical paragraph and sketch a picture of yourself. Write a topic sentence that includes your name and a general statement about your three items. For example, *My name is Geoff Hetzel and I enjoy being outside.* Expand on the ideas you wrote on the Autobiographical Brainstorm transparency by adding more details. For example, *I enjoy riding my mountain bike in the Levitt Forest. I love to build model rockets and launch them in my backyard. My friends and I like to play flag football on weekends.* Write a closing statement that restates the main idea. For example, *These three activities are what I enjoy the most.*

Guided Practice

1 Invite a volunteer to share his or her three objects again. Ask the volunteer to explain how each object represents his or her life.

2 Give each student an Autobiographical Brainstorm reproducible. Invite students to write a topic sentence, three detail sentences, and a closing statement based on the information the volunteer shared.

3 Divide the class into small groups. Have students read aloud each sentence to their group. Encourage students in each group to help the author revise and edit the sentences.

Independent Practice

1 Give each student another Autobiographical Brainstorm reproducible. Invite students to write their own autobiographical statement, including three detail sentences based on their objects.

2 Have students write a rough draft paragraph on lined paper. Remind them to expand on the ideas they recorded on their Autobiographical Brainstorm reproducible by adding details to each sentence. Encourage more advanced writers to write a paragraph about each object.

3 Have students revise and edit their rough draft and then use the rubric to evaluate their writing.

● Have students **publish** their final drafts on the writing template reproducible. Have them draw an illustration or tape a photograph in the frame at the top of the page.

● **Display** student work mounted on colored construction paper on a bulletin board titled *Mirror, Mirror.* Use aluminum foil for the background of the bulletin board, and place small mirrors along the edges.

TEACHING HINTS/EXTENSIONS

● Invite students to bring in a bag with several objects and write a paragraph about how, where, and when they got each object.

● Ask students to write riddles about themselves as a new way of writing an autobiography.

● Have students take on the role of a fictional character, scientist, or historical figure. Encourage them to write a short autobiographical piece based on what they know about the person.

● Have students complete one or more of these writing prompts in a journal:
   ✔ Write an autobiographical paragraph about your life before you were old enough to go to school. Tell at least three things that you remember.
   ✔ Write an autobiographical paragraph as if you were a famous singer, dancer, or musician.
   ✔ Imagine you are a rain forest animal. Write an autobiographical paragraph about your life.

Autobiographical Brainstorm

Topic Sentence (Who is this paragraph about?)

_____

_____

Detail Sentence #1 (Object One)

_____

_____

Detail Sentence #2 (Object Two)

_____

_____

Detail Sentence #3 (Object Three)

_____

_____

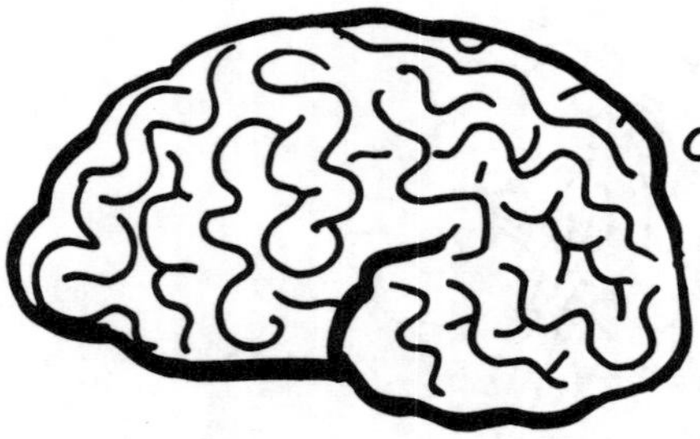

Closing Statement (Restate the main idea.)

_____

_____

Steps to Writing Success: Level 2 © 2002 Creative Teaching Press

By

Steps to Writing Success: Level 2 © 2002 Creative Teaching Press

Pictures from the Past

Preparation

Read aloud short biographical stories.

- *Mary McLeod Bethune* by Eloise Greenfield (HarperCollins)
- *Peter the Great* by Diane Stanley (William Morrow & Company)
- *A Picture Book of Helen Keller* by David A. Adler (Holiday House)

Invite a member of the school staff (e.g., principal, secretary, nurse) to the classroom to be interviewed.

Gather a clipboard for each student, and use string to tie a pencil to it.

Create a microphone by taping a ball of foil to an empty toilet paper roll.

Write and send home a parent letter to explain that students are learning about interviews and writing biographical paragraphs. Tell parents that students will have two to three days to interview a relative (on the telephone or in person).

Make copies of these reproducibles.
- Interview Sheet (page 117) four transparencies, two class sets of photocopies
- All About (page 118) transparency, class set of photocopies
- rubric (page 8) class set of photocopies

Setting the Stage

Invite three volunteers to take on the role of older relatives to be interviewed. Display an Interview Sheet overhead transparency. Ask each volunteer the questions, and record each student's responses on a separate transparency. Invite volunteers to hold the toy microphone when they answer the questions.

OBJECTIVE

The student will interview a relative and write a biographical paragraph about that person.

CRITICAL COMPONENTS

- The paragraph includes a topic sentence with the relative's name.

- The paragraph includes at least three details about the relative's life.

- The paragraph includes a closing statement that summarizes the relative's life.

Instructional Input

1 Discuss what interviews are and what their purpose is. Emphasize that interviews are used to gather information about a person and that careful notes must be taken.

2 Interview a member of the school staff. Ask a question, listen to the response, and ask the class to tell you what to record on an Interview Sheet transparency. Repeat this process for each question.

3 Display the All About overhead transparency. Model how to write a paragraph about the staff member based on his or her responses.

Guided Practice

1 Give each student a clipboard and an Interview Sheet reproducible. Invite students to work with a partner to conduct a practice interview. Encourage them to take on the role of an imaginary older relative.

2 Ask partners to take turns asking questions. Remind them to listen carefully and write a lot of notes.

3 Invite students to share information about their interview with the class. Have them share the name and relationship of the person they interviewed and his or her response to one of the questions.

Independent Practice

1 Give each student a clipboard and another Interview Sheet reproducible. Have students take these items home to use when they interview a relative. Encourage students to call relatives who live in a different state on the telephone. Provide two to three days for students to conduct their interview and bring their materials back to school.

2 Have students work in class to write a paragraph based on the information they recorded on their Information Sheet.

3 Have students revise and edit their rough draft and then use the rubric to evaluate their writing.

Presentation

- Have students **publish** their final drafts on the All About reproducible. Have them draw an illustration or tape a photograph in each frame.

- Invite students to **present** their biographical paragraphs to the class and invited guests (the relatives students interviewed, if possible).

- **Create** a photo album or scrapbook by mounting each student's paragraph on a piece of construction paper. Encourage students to decorate the back of their construction paper page with drawings or photographs of the relative. Bind together the pages. (Take the book apart and distribute the pages to students at the end of the year.)

TEACHING HINTS/EXTENSIONS

- Videotape clips of television interviews from the news, and play them for the class. These clips will help students internalize interview etiquette.

- Host a career day or week. Invite several guests who work in different careers to visit the classroom. Have students prepare interview questions, interview each guest, and share what they learned about different careers.

- Invite students to develop puppet plays with classroom puppets or home-made puppets. Encourage them to use the puppets to hold interviews.

- Have students complete one or more of these writing prompts in a journal:
  - ✔ Write a biographical paragraph about a character in your favorite story.
  - ✔ Write a paragraph about the life of a favorite pet.
  - ✔ Imagine you could interview a cartoon character, such as Mickey Mouse, Donald Duck, or Daffy Duck. Write interview questions to ask this character.

Interview Sheet

Name of Relative: _____

Relationship to You: _____

Question #1
Do you have special memories of your childhood? Can you describe them to me?

_____

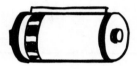

Question #2
Do you have special memories of your teenage years? Can you describe them to me?

_____

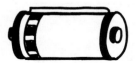

Question #3
Do you have special memories of things you and I did together? Can you describe them to me?

_____

_____

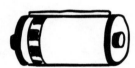

Question #4
Is there anything else you would like to tell me?

_____

_____

All About _____

By_____

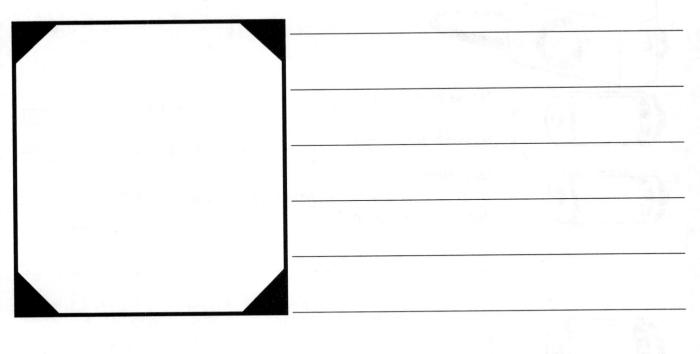

_____

_____

_____

_____

_____

_____

_____

_____

_____

_____

_____

_____

Steps to Writing Success: Level 2 © 2002 Creative Teaching Press

Once Upon a Time

Preparation

Read aloud short fictional stories.

- *Hansel and Gretel* by Rika Lesser (Dutton)
- *Lon Po Po: A Red Riding Hood Story from China* by Ed Young (Philomel)
- *Saint George and the Dragon* by Margaret Hodges (Little, Brown and Company)

Gather four different colored pencils for each student and four different colored overhead pens.

Make copies of these reproducibles.
- A Giant and a Wolf (page 122) transparency, class set of photocopies
- Story Frame (page 123) transparency, one photocopy for every two students
- Story Map (page 124) class set of photocopies
- writing template (page 125) two to three class sets of photocopies
- rubric (page 8) class set of photocopies

CRITICAL COMPONENTS

- The story tells the characters' names and describes their personalities.

- The story describes the setting.

- The story has a conflict and a resolution.

Setting the Stage

Define and discuss key literary terms related to short stories, such as setting, characters, conflict, and resolution. Discuss some of the stories read during the preceding week. Ask students to identify the setting, characters, conflict, and resolution of each story. Display the A Giant and a Wolf overhead transparency, give each student a reproducible, and read it aloud. Review the key literary terms by asking students to find the setting, characters, conflict, and resolution in the story. Assign each literary term a different color, and have students underline the parts of the story that represent each literary term with a different colored pencil on their paper. Then, invite volunteers to underline this information on the transparency with different colored overhead pens.

Instructional Input

1 Display the Story Frame overhead transparency. Read it aloud with the blanks.

2 Ask students to suggest possible settings, characters, conflicts, resolutions, and positive and negative personality characteristics for the story. Record their responses on the board.

3 Invite the class to choose one setting, two characters, three conflicts, three resolutions, one positive personality characteristic, and one negative personality characteristic from the list on the board.

4 Fill in the blanks with the appropriate words the class chose. Read aloud the completed story.

Guided Practice

1 Divide the class into pairs. Invite students to work with a partner to write their own story. Give each pair a Story Frame reproducible. Tell students to write on the back of their paper or on a separate piece of paper a list of possible settings, characters, conflicts, resolutions, and positive and negative personality characteristics for their story.

2 Have partners work together to fill in the blanks of their story with words from their list. Tell them to circle the words on their list and then write them in the blanks.

3 Invite partners to read aloud their story to the class.

Independent Practice

1 Invite students to write their own short story that includes a setting, at least two characters, a conflict, and a resolution. Give each student a Story Map reproducible, and have students record the basic information for their story.

2 Ask students to write a rough draft of their short story by expanding on the information they recorded on their Story Map reproducible.

3 Have students revise and edit their rough draft and then use the rubric to evaluate their writing.

Presentation

- Have students **publish** their final drafts and illustrations on several writing template reproducibles.

- Invite students to **create** front and back construction paper covers and bind together their pages with staples or yarn.

- **Display** the books in the school library or classroom library.

TEACHING HINTS/EXTENSIONS

- Divide the class into groups of three to five students. Invite them to become traveling authors and visit other classrooms to read aloud their stories. This modeling is great inspiration for younger students and builds confidence for the authors.

- Create an area of your classroom specifically for student-authored texts. As the number of books grows, divide them into magazine racks with labels such as *Adventure Stories, Fairy Tales, Tall Tales, Fables, Poetry,* and *Nonfiction.*

- Check your local bookstore for a copy of *The Ultimate Guide to Student Contests, Grades K–6* by Scott Pendleton (Walker). As you notice clever story development in students' writing, consider entering their work with parental permission. You may also wish to design writing assignments around specific contests.

- Have students complete one or more of these writing prompts in a journal:
    - ✔ Write a story about a tortoise that refused to come out of its shell.
    - ✔ Write a story about a child who would not go to bed.
    - ✔ Write a story about an elephant that rescued a lost child.

A Giant and a Wolf

Once upon a time a giant and a wolf lived in a beautiful wooded forest. The giant was mean and hated the forest animals, but the wolf was kind to all the forest animals. The problem was that the giant tried to take over the entire forest and make all the animals miserable.

First, the giant tried to cut down all the trees, but the wolf stopped him. The wolf had the woodpeckers warn all the other forest animals of his evil plan, and they blocked his path so he couldn't enter the forest.

Then, the giant tried to dam up the entire river so the animals wouldn't have water, but the wolf stopped him from being successful. The wolf told the beavers to chew up the dam so the water would flow again.

After that, the giant tried to burn down the forest, but the wolf stopped him. The wolf asked the rain clouds for help. They created a storm that put out the fire.

Finally, the giant gave up and decided to be nice. The forest animals lived happily ever after and the wolf was king.

Steps to Writing Success: Level 2 © 2002 Creative Teaching Press

Names _____ _____ Date _____

Story Frame

Once upon a time there lived _____ and
(character #1)

_____ . They lived in a _____ .
(character #2)   (setting)

_____ was _____
(character #1)   (positive personality characteristic)

and _____ was _____ .
(character #2)   (negative personality characteristic)

The problem was that _____
(major problem)

_____ .

First, _____ ,
(problem that character #2 caused)

but then _____
(action of character #1 that resolved the problem

_____ .

After that, _____ ,
(problem that character #2 caused)

but then _____
(action of character #1 that resolved the problem)

_____ .

Finally, _____ ,
(problem that character #2 caused)

but then _____
(action of character #1 that resolved the problem)

_____ .

Name _____   Date _____

Story Map

Title: _____

Setting: _____

_____

Characters: _____

_____

_____

Conflict (Problem): _____

_____

_____

Resolution (Solution): _____

_____

_____

Steps to Writing Success: Level 2 © 2002 Creative Teaching Press

By

Walkie-Talkie

Preparation

Read aloud books that use dialogue.

- *Frog and Toad Together* by Arnold Lobel (HarperCollins)
- *George and Martha: The Complete Stories of Two Best Friends* by James Marshall (Houghton Mifflin)
- *Oliver* by Syd Hoff (HarperCollins)

Gather three colored pencils for each student, two homemade or purchased puppets, a small toy that one puppet can carry, and three different colored overhead pens.

Make copies of these reproducibles.
- Walkie-Talkie Dialogues (page 129) transparency, class set of photocopies
- writing template (page 130) transparency, class set of photocopies
- rubric (page 8) class set of photocopies

Setting the Stage

Introduce the two puppets to the class. Tell students to be quiet so the puppets aren't scared and so their conversation can be heard. Have Puppet #2 leave and come back carrying a small toy. Have the puppets act out the following skit, and then put them away.

Puppet #1: "Hey, what do you have in your hand?"
Puppet #2: "My toy."

Puppet #1: "That's not your toy."
Puppet #2: "Yes, it is!"

Puppet #1: "No, it is not. I lost that toy yesterday."
Puppet #2: "Well, I found the toy yesterday."

Puppet #1: "But it's mine!"
Puppet #2: "It is not."

Puppet #1: "Is too."
Puppet #2: "Finders keepers, losers weepers."

Puppet #1: "I'm going to tell the teacher."
Teacher: "You two need to stop arguing. I'm going to talk to the class and see how they think you should handle this problem. Right now, you two will have to be quiet."

OBJECTIVE

The student will write a dialogue between two characters.

CRITICAL COMPONENTS

- The dialogue has quotation marks around spoken words and phrases.

- A capital letter begins each quote.

- The line is indented each time a new character speaks.

Instructional Input

1 Discuss how the conversation between the two puppets turned into an argument. Ask the class what "Finders keepers, losers weepers" means. Invite the class to come up with a solution for the puppets' problem.

2 Invite students to help you create a conversation that the puppets might have that will help them solve their problem.

3 Record the conversation on the writing template overhead transparency. Use a different color overhead pen for each speaker rather than writing *Puppet #1* and *Puppet #2*. Writing with two different colors will help students determine who is speaking. Do not write the quotation marks at this time. Remember to indent for each speaker. Begin with Puppet #1's part. For example, the class might make up a conversation like this:

When you find something, you should turn it into the Lost and Found.

I did that before and nobody ever came and got it.

What happened then?

The lost and found people gave me the basketball after three days because nobody claimed it.

Well, sometimes people do come back and claim what they've lost.

Oh. Does that happen a lot?

Yes. Plus you have to remember that that toy means something special to me. My uncle bought it for me and I don't see him very often.

Oh, I'm sorry.

Will you give the toy back to me?

Yes. I'm sorry. I will use the Lost and Found next time.

4 Ask students what quotation marks are and what they are used for. Explain that when someone records a conversation on paper they should place quotation marks around what each person said.

5 Have students help you use an overhead pen in a third color to place quotation marks around each puppet's dialogue in the conversation you recorded on the transparency. Bring back the puppets to present the conversation.

Guided Practice

1 Display the Walkie-Talkie Dialogues overhead transparency, and give each student a reproducible. Explain that the two conversations represent two children talking on walkie-talkies.

2 Ask two students to read aloud the dialogues. Assign different colors for capital letters, ending punctuation, and quotation marks, and have students use colored pencils to make corrections on their reproducible.

3 Invite volunteers to make corrections to each line of dialogue on the transparency. Have them use different colored overhead pens for capital letters, ending punctuation, and quotation marks. Ask students to check their own paper to see that they corrected all the mistakes.

Independent Practice

1 Invite students to brainstorm topics for dialogues (e.g., a mother and daughter talking about baking cupcakes, two friends talking about what they will play after school), and record their suggestions on the board.

2 Ask each student to write a dialogue between two characters. Tell students to write with two different colored pencils to distinguish between the two characters. Remind them to indent each time a new character speaks. Have them add quotation marks to the dialogue after they finish their rough draft.

3 Have students revise and edit their rough draft and then use the rubric to evaluate their writing.

Presentation

- Have students **publish** their final drafts on the writing template reproducible.

- **Invite** students to each create two paper bag puppets.

- Encourage students to **present** their dialogue by performing it for the class with their puppets.

TEACHING HINTS/EXTENSIONS

- Set up a puppet theater in the classroom. Invite students to use classmates' dialogues to perform puppet plays.

- Familiarize students with the Punch and Judy puppets that are popular in England. Invite students to create and perform dialogues.

- Invite students to write dialogue scripts for their favorite TV shows.

- Have students complete one or more of these writing prompts in a journal:
  - ✔ Write a conversation between a dog and a cat.
  - ✔ Record a dialogue between two ants at a picnic.
  - ✔ Write a conversation between two sharks in the middle of the ocean.

Walkie-Talkie Dialogues

Directions: Make corrections to these conversations. Add capital letters, ending punctuation, and quotation marks where they belong.

Conversation #1

Timmy, can you play today

Yes, can you

Yes. Let's go to mary jo's house

Okay. Hurry. Over and out.

roger

Conversation #2

hello are you there?

i am here. are you?

Come over and play with me.
I am at the park.

Okay I'm on my way. Over and out.

roger

Name _____   Date _____

_____

_____

_____

_____

_____

_____

_____

_____

_____

_____

_____

_____

Dialogue Dynamics

Preparation

Read aloud books that include dialogue with speaker tags.

- *A Million Fish . . . More or Less* by Patricia C. McKissack (Random House)
- *Sam Johnson and the Blue Ribbon Quilt* by Lisa Campbell Ernst (William Morrow & Company)
- *Stellaluna* by Janell Cannon (Harcourt)

Collect several cartoon strips from the newspaper. Use correction fluid to delete the dialogue, and make an overhead transparency of the cartoons.

Gather chart paper.

Make copies of these reproducibles.
- Cartoon Dialogue (page 134) transparency
- Cat and Mouse Dialogue (page 135) class set of photocopies
- writing template (page 136) transparency, two class sets of photocopies
- rubric (page 8) class set of photocopies

OBJECTIVE

The student will write a dialogue between two characters that includes quotation marks and descriptive speaker tags.

CRITICAL COMPONENTS

- The dialogue has quotation marks around spoken words and phrases.

- A capital letter begins each quote.

- The line is indented each time a new character speaks.

- Each line of dialogue includes a speaker tag that captures the emotion of the speaker.

Setting the Stage

Display the overhead transparency of cartoon strips. Ask students what they think is happening to the cartoon characters. Point out that the speech bubbles are for the words the characters are saying but that the words are missing. Ask the class to imagine what the characters are saying to each other. Invite several volunteers to share their ideas, and record them in the empty speech bubbles.

Instructional Input

1 Display the Cartoon Dialogue overhead transparency, and invite two students to read aloud the dialogue. Then, ask students what would happen if the speech bubbles were not there. Discuss how the characters' conversation could be shown. Remind students that they can write the dialogue and add quotation marks. Point out that if they look closely at this cartoon they can "see" a lot of emotion. Ask how the characters are feeling and how the students know this. (The illustration shows their emotions.) Discuss how the reader would know how the characters were feeling if there were no illustrations.

2 Explain to the class that when they write a dialogue and use quotation marks, they should use speaker tags (e.g., *shouted Ted, responded Lisa*) to show who is speaking and how he or she is speaking. Invite students to brainstorm speaker tags (e.g., *stated, asked, whispered, cried*), and record their responses on chart paper.

3 Display the writing template overhead transparency. Write the dialogue from the Cartoon Dialogue transparency. Include quotation marks. For each line of dialogue, draw in the box a small picture of the character that is speaking. Invite students to add a speaker tag to each line. For example, a revised line might be *"I'm excited," said Ted gleefully. "I'm going to meet my friend Regina to play soccer," he explained.* Discuss how the use of speaker tags and descriptive words and phrases helped show the emotions of the characters.

Guided Practice

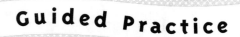

1 Give each student a Cat and Mouse Dialogue reproducible. Divide the class into pairs. Invite students to work with a partner to fill in the speech bubbles. Ask them to talk about what is happening in each scene of the cartoon before they write their dialogue.

2 Invite partners to share their dialogue with other partners to make sure the cartoon makes sense.

Independent Practice

1 Give each student a writing template reproducible. Have students translate the text they recorded in the speech bubbles on their Cat and Mouse Dialogue reproducible into written dialogue. Remind students to use quotation marks and indent when each new character speaks.

2 For each line of dialogue, have students sketch in the box a small picture of the character that is speaking. Remind them that this is a rough draft and therefore they should not spend too much time with the sketches. Have students add speaker tags and descriptive words and phrases to show the emotions of the characters.

3 Have students revise and edit their rough draft and then use the rubric to evaluate their writing.

P r e s e n t a t i o n

- Have students **publish** their final drafts on a second copy of the writing template reproducible.

- Invite students to **present** their dialogues by role-playing the skits with a partner.

- **Display** student work on a bulletin board titled *Dynamic Dialogues*.

TEACHING HINTS/EXTENSIONS

- Invite students to make cat and mouse puppets to use when they present their dialogues. Have them use paper bags or glue construction paper characters to craft sticks.

- Display the speaker tag word bank as a reference for students when they write. Encourage students to add to the word bank specific alternatives for more generic speaker tags. For example, students might add *yelled, announced, hissed, whispered, screamed,* and *cheerfully sang* to replace *said.*

- Set up a learning center for "dialogue duos." Cut out magazine pictures of character faces, and glue two faces on an index card. Place several cards in a decorated coffee can at the learning center. Invite students to choose a card and write a dialogue between the two characters based on the pictures on the card. Extend the activity by asking students to turn their dialogues into stories.

- Have students complete one or more of these writing prompts in a journal:
  - ✔ Write a dialogue with speaker tags about a conversation between two bears that want to hibernate in the same cave that only has room for one bear.
  - ✔ Write a dialogue with speaker tags about a conversation between two friends who forgive each other after they have had a terrible argument.
  - ✔ Write a dialogue with speaker tags about a conversation between two astronauts during their first flight into outer space.

Cartoon Dialogue

Name _____   Date _____

Cat and Mouse Dialogue

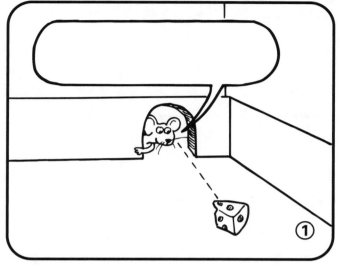

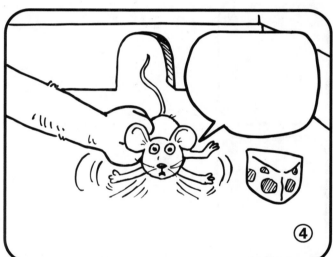

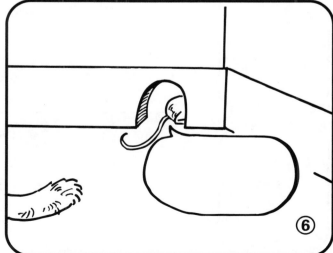

Name _____   Date _____

_____

_____

_____

_____

_____

_____

_____

_____

_____

_____

_____

_____

Steps to Writing Success: Level 2 © 2002 Creative Teaching Press

Ordering Arguments

Preparation

Read aloud books that will serve as good examples of how to order arguments.

- *Arthur Writes a Story* by Marc Tolon Brown (Little, Brown and Company)
- *Bedtime for Frances* by Russell Hoban (HarperCollins)
- *The Case of the Shrunken Allowance* by Joanne Rocklin (Cartwheel Books®)

Gather three pieces of chart paper.

Make copies of these reproducibles.
- Allowance Argument (page 140) one photocopy for every two students
- Ordering Arguments (page 141) class set of photocopies
- writing template (page 142) class set of photocopies
- rubric (page 8) class set of photocopies

Setting the Stage

Ask students to make a list of three or four things they would buy if they had more money of their own. Invite students to share one item from their list. Write these items on the board. Tell students that they are going to learn how to write persuasive paragraphs to convince others to listen to their opinions. Explain that they will develop their arguments and organize them in a special way. Explain that a persuasive paragraph has a beginning, middle, and ending just like a story. Tell students that in the beginning, the writer states his or her opinion; in the middle, the writer selects three reasons that support the opinion; and in the ending, the writer restates his or her opinion. Record this structure on chart paper. Ask volunteers to share three arguments they would give to convince their parents to help them purchase an item from their list.

Instructional Input

1 Have students share one reason they might give their parents for wanting a raise in their allowance. Record their responses on another piece of chart paper.

2 Invite students to work with a partner. Give each pair an Allowance Argument reproducible. Tell partners to fold their paper in half so they can only read the arguments (not the paragraph). Have partners decide what the correct order of the arguments should be and number them from 1 to 3.

3 Give partners time to report the order they chose for their arguments and defend the reasons for their choices. Tell students that the most important argument should go last for emphasis and the weakest one in the middle. Have the class use this rule to vote on an order for the arguments.

4 Invite the class to help you write a persuasive paragraph based on these arguments and the ones you recorded on the chart paper. Remind students that they need to write a topic sentence and a closing statement.

5 Ask students to unfold their Allowance Argument reproducible and read along as volunteers take turns reading aloud the paragraph. Compare this paragraph to the one the class wrote.

Guided Practice

1 Take an informal survey of what time students go to bed on weeknights and on weekends. Invite students to share reasons why they should be allowed to stay up 30 minutes later at night. Record their responses on another piece of chart paper.

2 Give each student an Ordering Arguments reproducible. Invite students to write three reasons why they should be allowed to stay up 30 minutes later at night. Encourage them to use the list on the chart paper as a guide, but ask them to develop their own arguments.

3 Have students look at their reasons and number them from 1 to 3 to show the order they should be stated in a persuasive paragraph. Remind them that the most important or strongest argument should be written last and the weakest argument should be written in the middle.

Independent Practice

1 Have students write their own persuasive paragraph based on the three reasons they wrote on their Ordering Arguments reproducible. Remind them to write a topic sentence and a closing statement and to be sure they state their reasons in the correct order. Encourage students to use the paragraph written by the class and the one on the Allowance Argument reproducible as guides as they write.

2 Have students revise and edit their rough draft and then use the rubric to evaluate their writing.

- Have students **publish** their final drafts on the writing template reproducible.

- Invite students to **present** their paragraphs. Ask the class to discuss whether they would be convinced to let the writer stay up later and explain why.

- **Display** student work on a bulletin board titled *Powerful Persuasion*.

TEACHING HINTS/EXTENSIONS

- Have students conduct surveys of at least ten students in their grade level to find out what time they go to bed. Remind students that they can use information about how other families schedule bedtime to construct an argument to persuade their parents to make their bedtime later.

- Use the information students compiled from the surveys to make a graph that shows how many students go to bed at various times.

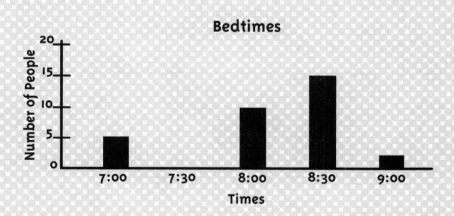

- Ask students to make a list of five things that they do every day. Have them write each task on a separate index card. Ask them to try to arrange a classmate's cards in order of the importance of each task.

- Have students complete one or more of these writing prompts in a journal:
    - ✔ Write a paragraph with three arguments to support why you want to see a new movie.
    - ✔ Write a paragraph with three arguments to support why your class should go on a particular field trip.
    - ✔ Write a paragraph with three arguments to support why you should pack your own lunch.

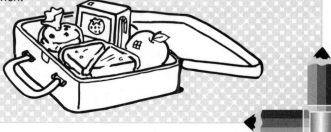

 # Allowance Argument

Order

	Opinion: I think I should get a raise in my allowance. Reason: I have been doing more work around the house to help the family.
	Opinion: I think I should get a raise in my allowance. Reason: I have been saving my money for a new bike, and I have been careful not to waste it on things like candy.
	Opinion: I think I should get a raise in my allowance. Reason: My older brother got a raise in his allowance when he was my age.

Raise My Allowance

I believe that I should get a raise in my weekly allowance. I have many reasons to support my request. First, I have been saving my money for a new bike, and I have been very careful not to waste my money on things like candy. Another fact to consider is that when my older brother was my age, he was given a raise in his allowance. Finally, I have been working around the house and doing extra chores to help the family. I hope that all of these reasons will help you to decide to give me a raise in my weekly allowance.

*Steps to Writing Success: Level 2* © 2002 Creative Teaching Press

Name _____   Date _____

Ordering Arguments

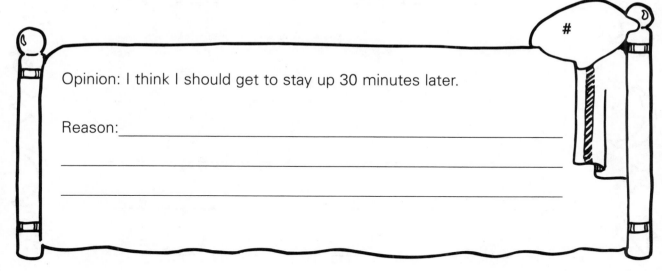

Opinion: I think I should get to stay up 30 minutes later.

Reason: _____

_____

_____

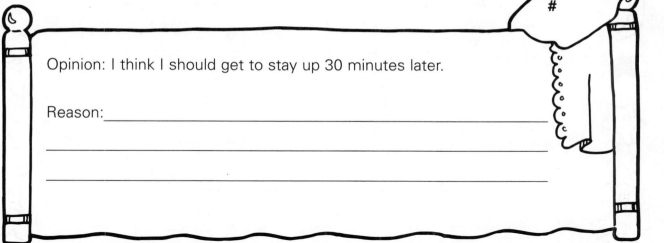

Opinion: I think I should get to stay up 30 minutes later.

Reason: _____

_____

_____

Opinion: I think I should get to stay up 30 minutes later.

Reason: _____

_____

_____

_____

By

_____

_____

_____

_____

_____

_____

_____

_____

_____

_____

_____

_____

Commercial Interruption

Preparation

Read aloud books about advertising or that have a product that can be advertised.

- *Nibble, Nibble, Jenny Archer* by Ellen Conford (Little, Brown and Company)
- *What a Character!: Twentieth Century American Advertising Icons* by Warren Dotz (Chronicle Books)
- *William's Doll* by Charlotte Zolotow (HarperCollins)

Videotape a variety of commercials, including ads for popular toys. Arrange to have a television and VCR in the classroom.

Make copies of these reproducibles.

- Sample Commercial Script (page 146) transparency
- Commercial Brainstorm (page 147) transparency, class set of photocopies
- Commercial Script (page 148) transparency, class set of photocopies
- rubric (page 8) class set of photocopies

Setting the Stage

Ask students if they have ever seen a commercial that convinced them that they wanted to buy that item just because of the commercial. Give each student time to share an example from his or her own experiences. Discuss what specific things the commercial did or said that made students want to buy the product. Guide the discussion, helping students to identify some of the effective strategies, such as a celebrity endorsement or words such as "new" and "improved." Play the video clips of commercials. Tell the class to listen carefully and look for ways that the commercial tries to convince the viewer to buy the product. Then, discuss the effective strategies that were used. Invite students to suggest ideas that would have made the commercials even more convincing.

OBJECTIVE

The student will write a television commercial to persuade an audience to buy a toy.

CRITICAL COMPONENTS

- The commercial uses persuasive words to convince the audience to buy the product.
- The commercial states at least three reasons why the product should be bought.
- The commercial uses a celebrity endorsement to appeal to the audience.

Instructional Input

1 Tell students that they are going to learn one of the ways that commercials often try to convince viewers that the product being advertised is the best product and that viewers should buy it immediately. Tell them this advertising technique is called celebrity endorsement. Explain to the class that commercials often use a famous person's name to help sell a product. Explain that advertisers hope that the recommendation of a famous person will make people more interested in buying the product. Give examples such as *Mike Hawk always buys Techno tennis shoes to jump higher on the court!* and *John Miller wins his competitions on a Wiley skateboard*. Once students understand the way this technique is used, invite them to share examples they have observed in commercials.

2 Display the Sample Commercial Script overhead transparency. Read it aloud, and then ask three volunteers to read each actor's part. Discuss the reasons this commercial might convince students to buy Crispy Critters cereal.

Guided Practice

1 Tell students that they are going to write a script for a television commercial to convince other children to buy their favorite toy. Remind them that commercials only last for 30 or 45 seconds, so they will have to quickly explain why the toy is something that viewers would want to own.

2 Ask students to suggest toys that they could write a commercial about. Record their suggestions on the board.

3 Display the Commercial Brainstorm overhead transparency. Invite the class to help you brainstorm ideas for a commercial for a toy that is endorsed by a famous person.

4 Display the Commercial Script overhead transparency. Ask students to assist you as you write the script for the commercial. Tell students that commercials may be written in a dialogue format like the Crispy Critters cereal example or as a paragraph to be read by one person.

Independent Practice

1 Invite students to write their own commercial for their favorite toy. Give each student a Commercial Brainstorm reproducible. Have students identify the name of the product, the setting for the commercial, reasons to buy the product, and a celebrity to endorse the product. (Display the Sample Commercial Script transparency for students to refer to for scaffolding.)

2 Give each student a Commercial Script reproducible, and invite students to write a rough draft of their commercial. Remind them to include all the information they recorded on the Commercial Brainstorm reproducible.

3 Have students revise and edit their rough draft and then use the rubric to evaluate their writing.

- Have students **publish** their final drafts on a poster-size piece of construction paper or tagboard so student "actors" can easily read them.

- Ask students to **present** their commercials and invite classmates to read the actors' parts.

- Invite students to **create** posters to advertise their products.

- **Display** student work around the school or at local stores.

TEACHING HINTS/EXTENSIONS

- Encourage students to use props, scenery, costumes, and background music to make their commercials appear more authentic when they act them out for the class. Videotape the presentations, and share them with other classes.

- After students view the videotaped television commercials, have them vote on the commercials that were most likely to persuade them to buy the product. Discuss why these commercials were more convincing than others. Present the results in a bar graph.

- Divide the class into groups of three to five students. Invite groups to choose an item to write a commercial about. Encourage them to write the commercial in a jingle or song format. Tell students that they can use the tunes to familiar songs such as "Twinkle, Twinkle Little Star" or "Row, Row, Row Your Boat."

- Have students complete one or more of these writing prompts in a journal:
  ✔ Write a commercial script for your favorite place to go on vacation.
  ✔ Write a commercial script for your favorite television show.
  ✔ Write a commercial script for your favorite flavor of ice cream.

Sample Commercial Script

Product: Crispy Critters Cereal

Setting: Kitchen
Situation: Billy does not want to try a new cereal.

Text of Commercial
   "Billy, it's time to eat your Crispy Critters!"
   "Aw, mom, I don't want to try a new cereal."

Just then, Billy looks up and sees his favorite basketball player, Jackie Johnson, standing in his kitchen.

   "Billy, don't you want to grow up to be big and strong like me?"

   "Yeah, Jackie!" Billy exclaims.

   "Well then, you need to eat your Crispy Critters cereal because it's an important part of a balanced breakfast."

   "I think it's a good idea for me to eat it."

Steps to Writing Success: Level 2 © 2002 Creative Teaching Press

Commercial Brainstorm

Product

Setting

Why should someone buy this product?

1. _____

2. _____

3. _____

This product is endorsed by

Commercial Script

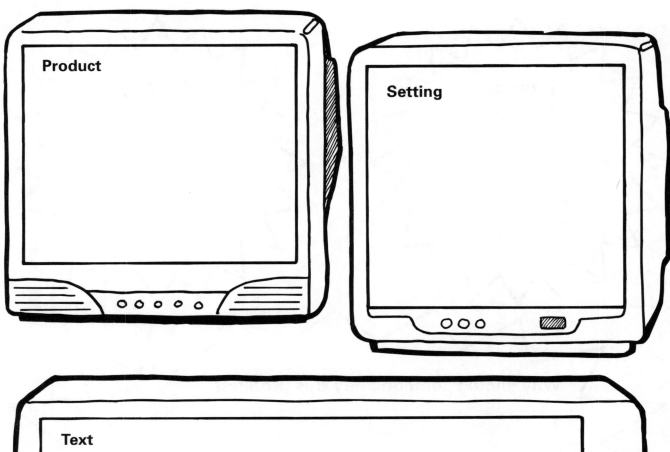

Product

Setting

Text

_____
_____
_____
_____
_____
_____
_____
_____

Steps to Writing Success: Level 2 © 2002 Creative Teaching Press

Big-Time Books

Preparation

Read aloud books that students can review.

- *The Day Jimmy's Boa Ate the Wash* by Trinka Hakes Noble (Penguin)
- *Dog Breath: The Horrible Trouble with Hally Tosis* by Dav Pilkey (Scholastic)
- *Mouse Soup* by Arnold Lobel (HarperCollins)

Discuss the books you read aloud, drawing specific attention to the setting and characters and encouraging students to summarize the story and express their personal opinions about each book.

Make copies of these reproducibles.
- Book Review Frame (page 152) transparency, class set of photocopies
- Sample Book Review (page 153) transparency
- writing template (page 154) transparency, class set of photocopies
- rubric (page 8) class set of photocopies

Setting the Stage

Invite students to describe some of the features that they feel are important to a good book, and record their responses on the board. Read aloud a book that you know will appeal strongly to your students' interests. Discuss some of the features that should be included in a book review, such as the title, characters, and what students liked and disliked. Invite volunteers to identify these features.

OBJECTIVE

The student will

write a book review.

CRITICAL COMPONENTS

- The topic sentence states the title and author of the book.

- The book review contains a brief summary of the book.

- The book review states reasons why the writer liked the book.

- The book review tells whether or not the writer recommends the book and explains why.

- The closing statement tells what the writer ranks the book (on a scale from 1 to 10).

Instructional Input

1 Display the Book Review Frame overhead transparency. Have each student tell one reason why he or she enjoyed the book you read aloud in Setting the Stage. Students might discuss the book's sense of humor, the main characters, the descriptions, or the ending. Record their responses on the board. Invite the class to vote on two or three reasons, and record them on the transparency.

2 Complete the transparency based on the book you read aloud. Ask the class to brainstorm ideas for a summary of the book, why they would or would not recommend it, and how they would rank it. Record their responses on the transparency.

3 Display the Sample Book Review overhead transparency, and read it aloud. Then, display the writing template overhead transparency. Use the information you recorded on the Book Review Frame to write a review of the book. Begin with a topic sentence that states the title and author of the book. End with a closing statement about whether or not you recommend the book, and give the book a ranking from 1 to 10.

Guided Practice

1 Invite students to choose a book from the classroom library or a book that they have recently read. Ask them to reread or review the book.

2 Divide the class into pairs. Have partners share the title, the author, and a summary of the book they read. Encourage students to tell their partner why they liked the book and the reasons why they would or would not recommend it.

3 Ask volunteers to share with the class the information their partner told them. Remind volunteers to share the title and author of the book, the reasons why their partner liked it, and why their partner would or would not recommend it.

Independent Practice

1 Give each student a Book Review Frame reproducible. Ask students to fill in information based on the book they shared with their partner.

2 Invite students to use the information they recorded on the Book Review Frame reproducible to write a book review. Remind students to begin their paragraph with a topic sentence that states the title and author of the book and end with a closing statement that tells whether or not they recommend the book and gives the book a ranking from 1 to 10.

3 Have students revise and edit their rough draft and then use the rubric to evaluate their writing.

Presentation

- Have students **publish** their final drafts and illustrations on the writing template reproducible.

- **Display** student work on a bulletin board titled *Recommended Reading*.

TEACHING HINTS/EXTENSIONS

- Have the class create a television talk show designed to review children's books. Select a student to be the talk show host. Let other students share their reviews in front of the class as if they were professional book reviewers or authors.

- Show students how to use the Internet. Teach them to research background information on the author of a book and how to use a search engine to do a keyword search to find books on similar topics.

- Encourage students to read their books to their family. Have them ask their family members questions to see if they agree with the student's opinion of the book.

- Have students complete one or more of these writing prompts in a journal:
    - ✔ Write a book review of one of your favorite fairy tales.
    - ✔ Write a book review of a book about an animal.
    - ✔ Write a book review of a book that won an award (such as the Newbery Medal or Caldecott Award).

Book Review Frame

Title and Author

_____

_____

_____

_____

Summary

_____

_____

_____

_____

_____

_____

_____

_____

Reasons I Liked the Book

_____

_____

_____

_____

Why I Recommend (or Do Not Recommend) the Book

_____

_____

_____

_____

On a scale of 1 to 10, I would rank this book . . . (please circle your rating)

1   2   3   4   5   6   7   8   9   10

Could be better   Good   One of the best!

Steps to Writing Success: Level 2 © 2002 Creative Teaching Press

Sample Book Review

I read <u>Miss Spider's Tea Party</u> by David Kirk. Miss Spider wants the other bugs to come to her house for tea. They are all afraid of her and won't drink tea with her. Finally, they find out she is friendly. They all get along in the end. I like the pictures in this book. I also like the words that rhyme. I recommend this book because it is fun to read. I would give it a score of 9 because I think it was really great!

Steps to Writing Success: Level 2 © 2002 Creative Teaching Press

_____

By

_____

_____

_____

_____

_____

_____

_____

_____

Marvelous Movies

Preparation

Read aloud books about movies.

- *If You Take a Mouse to the Movies* by Laura Joffe Numeroff (HarperCollins)
- *Lights! Camera! Action Dog! (Wishbone Mysteries Series #11)* by Nancy Butcher (Lyrick Studios)
- *Penny Goes to the Movies* by Harriet Ziefert (Penguin Putnam)

Gather videotapes of familiar children's movies. Arrange to have a television and VCR in the classroom.

Make copies of these reproducibles.
- Movie Review Frame (page 158) transparency, class set of photocopies
- Sample Movie Review (page 159) transparency
- writing template (page 160) transparency, class set of photocopies

Setting the Stage

Lead a discussion about movies. Ask students where they like to go to see movies and what some of their favorite movies are. Give each student a chance to respond. Tell students that they are going to learn how to write a movie review. Ask students to name movie categories (e.g., western, comedy, drama). Record the categories as headings on the board. Ask students to name characteristics of each movie category (e.g., silly characters and jokes for comedy). Record the characteristics under the appropriate headings.

OBJECTIVE

The student will write a movie review.

CRITICAL COMPONENTS

- The topic sentence states the title of the movie and the movie category (genre).

- The movie review summarizes the plot of the movie and names the main characters.

- The movie review tells the writer's favorite scene and who would enjoy the movie.

- The closing statement tells whether or not the writer recommends the movie.

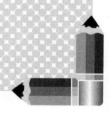

Instructional Input

1 Show some scenes from each of the children's movies you gathered. After showing the scenes, have students discuss the reasons why they liked or didn't like them. Encourage students to expand on their reasons with specific details.

2 Divide the class into small groups. Ask them to brainstorm some of the reasons why people like certain movies. Ask them to consider some of the things they like or don't like about movies. Assign one student in each group to be the recorder and write the group's ideas on a piece of paper.

3 Ask each group to report back to the class about the reasons they listed.

4 Choose one of the movies viewed in class to write a review about. Display the Movie Review Frame overhead transparency. Have the class help you fill in the information. Display the Sample Movie Review overhead transparency. Ask a volunteer to read it aloud. Discuss whether the review includes all the required components, and have volunteers circle or underline them.

5 Display the writing template overhead transparency. Invite the class to help you use the information you recorded on the Movie Review Frame to write a movie review. Begin the paragraph with a topic sentence that states the title and category (genre) of the movie, and end with a closing statement that tells whether or not you recommend the movie and why.

Guided Practice

1 Invite students to brainstorm children's movies that they enjoy watching. Limit the discussion to G- and PG-rated movies. Record their responses on the board.

2 Divide the class into pairs. Have partners choose from the list a movie that they both want to review. Give each student a Movie Review Frame reproducible.

3 Have partners work together to complete their own copy of the reproducible.

Independent Practice

1 Have each student use the information he or she recorded on the Movie Review Frame reproducible to write a movie review. Remind students to begin the paragraph with a topic sentence that states the title and category (genre) of the movie and end with a closing statement that tells whether or not they recommend the movie and why.

2 Have students revise and edit their rough draft and then use the rubric to evaluate their writing.

- Have students **publish** their final drafts on the writing template reproducible.

- Invite students to **present** their movie reviews. Encourage them to pretend they are movie critics.

- **Display** student work on a bulletin board titled *Take Me Out to the Movies*.

TEACHING HINTS/EXTENSIONS

- Encourage students to make movie posters or murals of their favorite movies, and display them around the classroom.

- Have students find out the average price of a movie theater ticket, a bag of popcorn or candy, and a soda. Have them work with a partner to add up the price per person for an evening at the movies.

- Invite students to write "movie riddles." A student could write *I had to live with a big hairy beast when my father made a mistake. I got to live in a castle and meet a dancing teapot and a singing candlestick. What movie am I in?* Challenge the class to answer the riddles. (*Disney's Beauty and the Beast*)

- Have students complete one or more of these writing prompts in a journal:
  - ✔ Write a review of your favorite animated film.
  - ✔ Think about a movie you didn't like. Write a review of it.
  - ✔ Write a paragraph about your favorite movie theater and explain why you like it.

Movie Review Frame

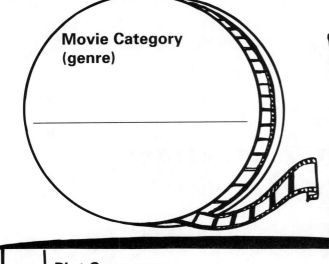

Movie Category (genre)

_____

Main Characters (actors)

_____

_____

_____

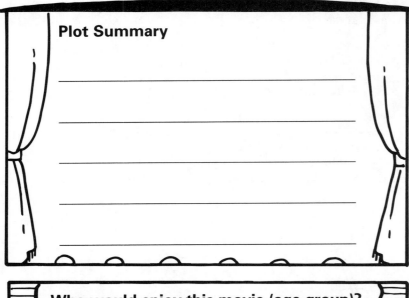

Plot Summary

_____

_____

_____

_____

_____

Favorite Scene

_____

_____

_____

_____

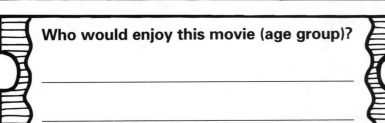

Who would enjoy this movie (age group)?

_____

_____

Recommendation

_____

_____

_____

Steps to Writing Success: Level 2 © 2002 Creative Teaching Press

Sample Movie Review

I like movies that are comedies. My favorite movie is "Willy Wonka and the Chocolate Factory." I watch it on video every Saturday. The movie is about kids going to Mr. Wonka's chocolate factory. They get to eat lots of candy and have many adventures. I like Charlie because he is nice, but I don't like the kids who get into lots of trouble. Mr. Wonka is mean at the beginning but nice at the end. The funniest part is when Barucha wants a golden egg. The machine thinks she is a bad egg, so she gets thrown into the garbage. All kids will like this movie because it is very funny. I think everyone should rent this movie immediately!

By

Steps to Writing Success: Level 2 © 2002 Creative Teaching Press

Restaurant Raves

Read aloud books about restaurants.

Preparation

- *Friday Night at Hodges' Café* by Tim Egan (Houghton Mifflin)
- *Hamburger Heaven* by Wong Herbert Yee (Houghton Mifflin)
- *Little Nino's Pizzeria* by Karen Barbour (Econo-Clad Books)

Assign each student one of these ethnic food groups/restaurants: Mexican, Italian, Asian, American.

Make copies of these reproducibles.
- parent letter (page 164) class set of photocopies
- Review Checklist (page 165) transparency, class set of photocopies
- Restaurant Review (page 166) transparency, class set of photocopies
- writing template (page 167) transparency, class set of photocopies
- rubric (page 8) class set of photocopies

Write the date of Restaurant Day (see Setting the Stage) and each student's restaurant on the parent letter (page 164), sign your name at the bottom, and send home the letter.

Setting the Stage

Host a Restaurant Day in the classroom. Divide the class into four groups based on the ethnic food groups you assigned them. Assign each group a corner of the classroom to set up their "restaurant." Ask groups to post a sign or banner with the name of their ethnic food group (i.e., Mexican, Italian, Asian, American) and decorate their corner of the classroom. Invite groups to set up their food selections and serve them to the rest of the class. Discuss the different types of food at each restaurant. Ask students what similarities and differences they noticed.

OBJECTIVE

The student will write a review of one of his or her favorite restaurants.

CRITICAL COMPONENTS

- The topic sentence states the name of the restaurant.
- The review tells about the décor, foods, and service at the restaurant.
- The closing statement tells why the writer recommends the restaurant.

Instructional Input

1 Tell students that they are going to write a restaurant review. Display the Review Checklist overhead transparency, and give each student a reproducible.

2 Read aloud the questions that describe some of the things that people are concerned about when they are choosing a restaurant. Fill in one of the columns together (using information about the "restaurants" from Setting the Stage), and then allow students to work in small groups to fill in the remaining columns on their own reproducible.

3 Have volunteers share some of the reasons why they would recommend a particular restaurant. Explain that writing a restaurant review involves identifying specific things that you enjoyed or liked and sharing them with the audience to convince them to accept your recommendation.

Guided Practice

1 Display the Restaurant Review overhead transparency. Choose a restaurant that the entire class knows, such as McDonalds, and record students' opinions.

2 Display the writing template overhead transparency. Invite the class to help you write a restaurant review. Tell students that each category from the Restaurant Review transparency should be reflected in a sentence in the restaurant review.

3 Read aloud the review, or ask volunteers to read it aloud. Give each student a Restaurant Review reproducible. Have students work with a partner to identify which sentence in the class's restaurant review corresponds to each box on the Restaurant Review reproducible. Invite students to share their answers with the class. (Ask students to keep the reproducible to use in Independent Practice.)

Independent Practice

1 Invite students to choose one of their favorite restaurants or a restaurant that they have visited recently with family or friends to write a review about. Have students complete their Restaurant Review reproducible.

2 Display the overhead transparency of the restaurant review written by the class as an example to provide scaffolding for students as they write.

3 Have students revise and edit their rough draft and then use the rubric to evaluate their writing.

● Have students **publish** their final drafts on the writing template reproducible and mount them on construction paper.

● Invite students to **present** their restaurant reviews to the class. Encourage them to pretend they are restaurant critics.

● **Display** student work on a bulletin board titled *A Restaurant the Rest-Will-Want.*

TEACHING HINTS/EXTENSIONS

● Invite students to design menus for the restaurants they set up during Setting the Stage. Encourage them to include additional food items that were not offered in the class activity. Have students list the price next to each food item and calculate how much it would cost them to order a meal.

SUN RISE

	$.95		$.99
	$1.25		$1.25
	$4.95		$2.50
	$2.50		$5.95
	$.85		$2.25
	$3.00		$3.00
			$4.50

● Ask students to bring in sample menus from a variety of restaurants. Review the components of a balanced meal, and address the food groups bodies need food from to achieve good nutrition. Ask students to "order" a meal that contains food from all the important food groups.

● Invite students to make 3-D models of their favorite dinners from a restaurant. Give them construction paper, pipe cleaners, glue, scissors, and paper plates. Display the dinners, and ask the class to identify each meal.

● Have students complete one or more of these writing prompts in a journal:
  ✔ Look at a restaurant's menu. Write a paragraph to persuade the restaurant to add more choices to the kids' menu.
  ✔ Write a paragraph to persuade your favorite restaurant to buy one of your mom's recipes and serve it at the restaurant.
  ✔ Write a paragraph to persuade a restaurant to give free dessert to kids who eat all their vegetables.

Date_____

Dear Parents,

Our class has been learning how to write persuasive reviews. This week we will be learning how to write a restaurant review. To create a more enjoyable experience for the students before they begin their writing activities, we will be organizing our class into four separate restaurant areas. Students will be assigned to one of four groups: Mexican restaurant, Italian restaurant, Asian restaurant, or American/Fast food restaurant. The groups will bring samples of food from their type of restaurant. Each group will have an opportunity to serve the class. Our Restaurant Day will be on

_____.

Please help support our activity by providing your child with a sample of food from his or her category. Your child's restaurant is _____. The foods listed below are merely suggestions; feel free to make substitutions of ethnic foods that you know would fit within the restaurant theme.

Mexican Food	**Italian Food**
chips and salsa tacos enchiladas quesadillas Spanish rice refried beans	garlic bread spaghetti pizza lasagna meatballs Italian ices
Asian Food	**American (Fast) Food**
fried rice steamed rice egg rolls chow mein fortune cookies orange chicken	french fries burgers milk shakes apple pie macaroni salad chocolate chip cookies

If you have any questions, please contact me. I appreciate your involvement in helping to make this an enjoyable experience for your child.

Sincerely,

Name _____   Date _____

Review Checklist

	Mexican Food	Italian Food	Asian Food	American Food
Was the food fresh?				
Was the food colorful?				
Was the service good?				
Was the restaurant décor attractive?				
Was the hot food hot?				
Was the cold food cold?				
Would you recommend this restaurant? Why?				

Name _____   Date _____

Restaurant Review

Name of Restaurant: _____

Restaurant décor and atmosphere: _____

_____

_____

Variety of foods to choose from: _____

_____

_____

Quality and taste of food: _____

_____

_____

Quality of service: _____

_____

_____

Why would you recommend this restaurant? _____

_____

_____

Steps to Writing Success: Level 2 © 2002 Creative Teaching Press

_____

By

_____

Steps to Writing Success: Level 2 © 2002 Creative Teaching Press

Invention Convention

Preparation

Read aloud books about inventors and inventions.

- *Ben and Me: An Astonishing Life of Benjamin Franklin* by Robert Lawson (Little, Brown and Company)
- *Great Black Heroes: Five Notable Inventors* by Wade Hudson (Scholastic)
- *A Picture Book of Thomas Alva Edison* by David A. Adler (Holiday House)

Gather advertisements from magazines and catalogs.

Create a three-column chart titled *You've Got to Buy This!* Label the columns *Clever Names, Descriptive Words and Phrases,* and *Persuasive Words and Phrases.*

Make copies of these reproducibles.
- Invention Information (page 171) transparency, class set of photocopies
- Homework-o-Matic (page 172) transparency
- writing template (page 173) transparency, class set of photocopies
- rubric (page 8) class set of photocopies

Setting the Stage

Divide the class into small groups. Challenge groups to list as many daily jobs (e.g., brushing teeth, combing hair, tying shoelaces, cleaning rooms) as they can. Write two to three ideas from each group on the board. Tell students that many of the inventions that were designed by famous people like Thomas Edison or Benjamin Franklin resulted because the inventors were trying to figure out a faster or easier way to get a job done. Invite students to choose one of the jobs or tasks from the list and think of an item they could invent that would do the job for them. For example, they could invent a robotic dog that sits under their chair at dinner and disposes of all their vegetables. Have students imagine that they had unlimited resources and money to design the invention. Have students draw a picture of the invention and write a sentence that tells what it will do. Collect these pictures to use in Independent Practice.

OBJECTIVE

The student will write an advertisement for an original invention.

CRITICAL COMPONENTS

- The advertisement features a clever name for the invention and its price.

- The advertisement describes the invention and how it will help people.

- The advertisement uses persuasive words and phrases to tell people why they should buy the invention.

1 Tell students that inventors have to let people know about their products so that they will want to buy them. Ask students how inventors do this. Discuss advertisements and how they help inventors promote their products.

2 Divide the class into small groups. Give each group several advertisements. Ask students to look for common elements in the advertisements, such as promises about what the product can do, descriptions of the product with interesting and appealing words, persuasive phrases to convince the reader to buy the product or to make the product sound affordable and necessary, and a clever or interesting product name.

3 Display the You've Got to Buy This! chart. Invite students to help you build a word bank they can use as a reference when they write their invention ads. Tell students to look at the advertisements and share clever names, descriptive words and phrases, and persuasive words and phrases. Record their responses on the chart.

You've Got to Buy This!

Clever Names	Descriptive Words and Phrases	Persuasive Words and Phrases
Crest®- Dual Action Whitening	removes stains, makes teeth white	unlike any ordinary toothpaste, new, introducing
Swiffer Wet™	Pre-moistened, disposable, advanced cleaning solution	…is the first, removes 95% of bacteria, changing, cleaning

1 Tell students that the class will create a new invention called the "Homework-o-Matic" that will take homework papers and complete them with the correct answers in the student's own handwriting in less than one minute per page. Ask how many students would buy this invention.

2 Display the Invention Information overhead transparency. Invite students to help you complete all the information about the Homework-o-Matic.

3 Display the writing template overhead transparency. Have students help you write an advertisement for the Homework-o-Matic based on the information you recorded on the Invention Information transparency. Invite a volunteer to draw an illustration at the bottom of the advertisement.

4 Display the Homework-o-Matic overhead transparency. Read aloud the sample advertisement. Ask volunteers to identify and circle sentences that show the name of the invention, how it will help people, descriptive words, persuasive words, and the price. Have students compare this advertisement to the one the class wrote, vote on which one is more persuasive, and explain the reasons why. (Optional: Invite the class to write another advertisement that combines parts from each ad to create the most persuasive advertisement.)

Independent Practice

1 Give students the invention picture they drew in Setting the Stage and an Invention Information reproducible.

2 Have students complete the reproducible based on their own invention.

3 Ask students to write an advertisement for their invention. Display the overhead transparency of the advertisement the class wrote about the Homework-o-Matic as an example.

4 Have students revise and edit their rough draft and then use the rubric to evaluate their writing.

Presentation

• Have students **publish** their final drafts and illustrations of their inventions on the writing template reproducible.

• **Display** student work on a bulletin board titled *Invention Convention*. Put pictures of famous inventors around the border.

TEACHING HINTS/EXTENSIONS

• Discuss the cost to produce the Homework-o-Matic and the price it would be sold for. Find the difference between the production price and the selling price to determine the profit for the inventor. Ask students to find the profit for their own inventions. Chart the profits on a line graph.

• Invite students to use their sketches to help them build a model of their invention. Give students art supplies, or have students bring them from home.

• Give students a list of famous inventors. Invite them to work in small groups to discover how one inventor got started. Encourage them to find as many details about the inventor's childhood as possible.

• Have students complete one or more of these writing prompts in a journal:
  ✔ Write an advertisement for a brand of dog food that cleans your dog's teeth.
  ✔ Write an advertisement for a new piece of playground equipment.
  ✔ Create an invention that will help you at school. Write an advertisement for it.

Invention Information

Name for my invention

_____

How my invention will help people

_____

_____

Descriptive words to make my invention sound appealing

_____ _____ _____

_____ _____ _____

Persuasive words to help convince people to buy my invention

_____ _____ _____

_____ _____ _____

Affordable price for my invention

_____

Homework-o-Matic

Students of all ages! You won't want to miss out on this amazing opportunity to get your own Homework-o-Matic! This handy little machine completes all your homework in less than one minute per page, and does it in your own personal handwriting! With the latest in technology, your homework will always be done efficiently and accurately. Act now, and you can get your own personal Homework-o-Matic for three low payments of only $7.95 each. Don't be left out—buy yours today!

Steps to Writing Success: Level 2 © 2002 Creative Teaching Press

_____

By

_____

Amusement Fun

Preparation

Read aloud books about amusement parks.

- *The Berenstain Bears Ride the Thunderbolt* by Stan and Jan Berenstain (Random House)
- *Horrible Harry and the Drop of Doom* by Suzy Kline (Viking)
- *Roller Coasters* by Nick Cook (Carolrhoda Books)

Collect from students photographs of themselves at an amusement park, a carnival, or a playground.

Create a three-column chart with the headings *Name of Park, Location,* and *Enjoyable Features.*

Make copies of these reproducibles.
- Evaluating Amusement Parks (page 177) transparency
- Amusement Park Word Banks (page 178) transparency, class set of photocopies
- writing template (page 179) transparency, class set of photocopies
- rubric (page 8) class set of photocopies

OBJECTIVE

The student will write a review of an amusement park, a carnival, or a playground.

CRITICAL COMPONENTS

- The topic sentence tells the name of the place.

- The paragraph describes the place.

- The closing statement tells whether or not the writer recommends the place.

Setting the Stage

Invite students to share their photographs and information about the amusement park, carnival, or playground and what they enjoyed about it. Display the chart you created. Record the names of the various parks, their locations, and the enjoyable features as students share their photographs and stories.

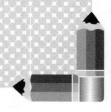

Instructional Input

1 Tell students that they are going to learn how to write a review of a specific amusement park.

2 Ask students to tell a partner four things he or she should know about an amusement park before deciding whether or not it is a good park to visit (e.g., rides, concessions, price, length of wait in line, cleanliness of park). Have volunteers share some of the areas they discussed, and write them on the board.

3 Display the Evaluating Amusement Parks overhead transparency. Choose an amusement park that the majority of students have visited, and complete the evaluation based on feedback from the students. Invite students to suggest other features they would evaluate, and write them in the blank spaces.

Guided Practice

1 Display the Amusement Park Word Banks overhead transparency, and give each student a reproducible. Have the class brainstorm words for each feature of the amusement park the class evaluated. Record the words on the transparency, and have students record them on their reproducible. This will provide scaffolding for students when they write their amusement park review.

2 Display the writing template overhead transparency. Invite students to help you write a review of the amusement park the class evaluated. Show students how to use words from the word banks to summarize their opinion of the various features of the amusement park.

Independent Practice

1 Have students write a review of the amusement park, carnival, or playground in their photograph. Remind students to describe it and tell whether or not they recommend it. Encourage them to include in their review persuasive and descriptive words from the word banks.

2 Have students revise and edit their rough draft and then use the rubric to evaluate their writing.

Presentation

- Have students **publish** their final drafts on the writing template reproducible.

- Invite students to **create** shoe box dioramas to illustrate the best ride at the amusement park, carnival, or playground they reviewed.

- **Display** student work and photographs on a bulletin board titled *Roll into Fun*. Place the dioramas on a table near the bulletin board.

TEACHING HINTS/EXTENSIONS

- Ask the school to purchase the computer software program Sim Theme Park by Electronic Arts. This program gives students the opportunity to create a theme park by selecting rides, shops, and concessions; setting the prices; and managing the inventory. Through the process of playing the game, they learn many business and mathematical principles.

- Choose a poetry pattern such as diamonte or haiku, and have students write poems about amusement parks. Have them design creative borders and illustrations for their poems, and display their poetry in a laminated class book.

- Invite students to plan imaginary trips to major amusement parks, such as Disney World. Have small groups work together to research the cost of travel by air, by train, or by car; the cost of hotel rooms; and the cost of meals and food for the trip.

- Have students complete one or more of these writing prompts in a journal:
  - ✔ Write a paragraph to persuade your favorite amusement park to add a new theme land to the park.
  - ✔ Write a paragraph about the job you would choose if you could work at your favorite amusement park.
  - ✔ Write a paragraph to the owner of a water park to persuade him or her to try to conserve water.

Evaluating Amusement Parks

Name of Amusement Park:_____

	Great	O.K.	Poor
Exciting rides			
Food selection at concession stands			
Length of time waiting in line for rides			
Cleanliness of the park			
Affordable admission price			
Theme-related activities or characters			

Amusement Park Word Banks

Words to Describe Rides

Words to Describe Food

Words to Describe the Park's Theme or Atmosphere

Words to Describe the Prices

Steps to Writing Success: Level 2 © 2002 Creative Teaching Press

By

Steps to Writing Success: Level 2 © 2002 Creative Teaching Press

Steps to Writing Success: Level 2 © 2002 Creative Teaching Press